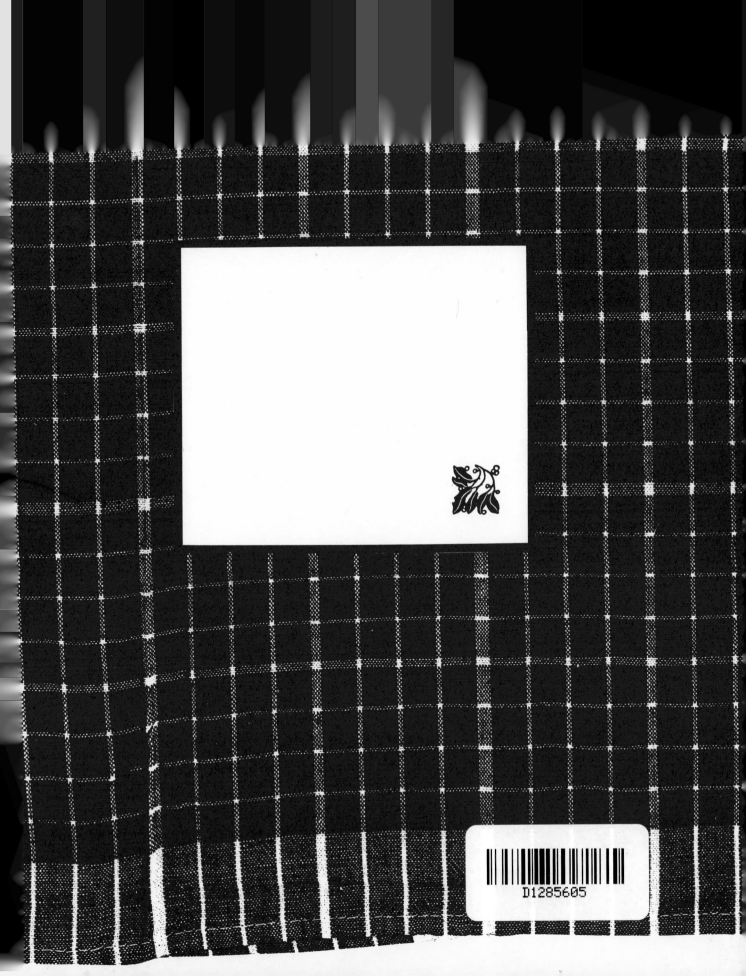

 LOGO DESIGN · SHELLEY SACHS · BOOK DESIGN · PHYLLIS DEMONG

The Bakery Lane Soup Bowl COOK BOOK

BY MARGE MITCHELL & JOAN SEDGWICK

LIBRARY OF CONGRESS CATALOGING-IN-PUBLICATION DATA

Mitchell, Marge.
   Bakery Lane Soup Bowl cookbook / by Marge Mitchell and Joan
      Sedgwick.
      p. cm.
   Originally published: Middlebury, Vt.: Bakery Lane Soup Bowl, 1976
   Includes index.
   ISBN 0-8397-1005-4
   1. Soups.   2. Salads.   3. Desserts.   4. Cookies   I. Sedgwick, Joan.
   II. Title.
TX757.M57   1993   93-8904
641.8'13--dc20   CIP

Foreword

THE FIRST EDITION OF THIS COOKBOOK WAS WRITTEN IN 1975 IN MIDDLEBURY, VERMONT, WHERE WE HAD RECENTLY OPENED A SMALL RESTAURANT CALLED THE BAKERY LANE SOUP BOWL. CUSTOMERS LOVED THE SOUP AND DESSERTS AT THE SOUP BOWL, WANTED THE RECIPES AND WE BLITHELY PROMISED A BOOK. IT QUICKLY BECAME EMBARRASSING TO ANSWER THE INEVITABLE QUESTION WITH "SOON." WE STARTED ON THE COOKBOOK, ALTERNATING POTATO PEELING AND WRITING. "SOON" BECAME "DONE!" WE WERE STUNNED WHEN THE BOOK WENT THROUGH THREE PRINTINGS IN A YEAR, AND THEN LATER WHEN IT WAS TAKEN FOR NATIONAL DISTRIBUTION.

MIDDLEBURY WAS CHARMING; THE SNOW WAS LESS SO. WE SOLD THE SOUP BOWL AND WITH THREE CATS AND A LARGE DOG IN A SMALL MOTOR HOME WE TREKKED WEST TO THE LAND OF LITTLE SNOW. DRIVING THROUGH PRESCOTT, ARIZONA, WE CAME UPON A GRASSY, SHADY TOWN SQUARE WITH THE COUNTY COURTHOUSE IN THE MIDDLE. IT LOOKED LIKE NEW

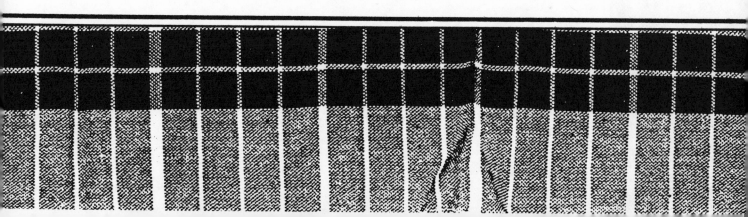

ENGLAND. WE QUICKLY OPENED A RESTAURANT ACROSS FROM THE SQUARE AND NAMED IT MAUDE AFTER A FAVORITE CAT. PRESCOTT WAS KIND TO US BUT WAS GROWING TOO FAST. SEARCHING ONCE AGAIN WE FELL IN LOVE WITH JEROME, A LITTLE MOUNTAIN TOWN IN NORTHERN ARIZONA—POPULATION 451. WE OPENED A NEW MAUDE'S AND DESPITE OUR LOCATION—DOWN A LITTLE SIDE STREET AND A FLIGHT OF STAIRS—THE TOURISTS FOUND US. OUR SECOND COOKBOOK, SOUP BOWL WEST, CAME OUT DURING THIS TIME.

CUSTOMERS WOULD OFTEN ASK WHO MAUDE WAS. THE NEXT TIME THEY VISITED THEY WOULD BRING A CAT POSTER OR CAT POT HOLDER, WHICH WE DISPLAYED. ANOTHER DINER WOULD TRY TO BUY THE CAT TOOTHPICK HOLDER. AS WE SAID NO, WE THOUGHT WHY NOT SELL CAT ITEMS IF THERE IS A DEMAND. WE OPENED A TINY CAT SHOP AND IT GREW INTO A LARGER SHOP ON MAIN STREET—MAUDE'S HOUSE OF CATS. TWO SHOPS WERE TOO MANY. WE SOLD THE

RESTAURANT AND NOW DEAL EXCLUSIVELY WITH CATS. EXCEPT, IF YOU DROP BY, AN OLD BLACK DOG NAMED JANE WILL COME OUT FROM BEHIND THE COUNTER TO SAY HELLO.

WE HAVE BEEN LUCKY. OUR RESTAURANTS AND OUR COOKBOOKS, ESPECIALLY THIS ONE, HAVE DONE WELL. WE TAKE HUMBLE CREDIT FOR THE GOOD FOOD WE SERVED. BUT WE MUST GIVE LOVING AND SINCERE CREDIT FOR THE SUCCESS OF THIS COOKBOOK TO FRIENDS WHO GAVE OF THEIR TIME TO READ AND MAKE SUGGESTIONS—AND ESPECIALLY OUR FRIEND, DESIGNER AND ILLUSTRATOR, PHYL DEMONG. HER SENSE AND GOOD TASTE ALWAYS PREVAILED.

MARGE AND JOAN
AND JANE AND EMMA AND ROBERT
REDFORD AND TRUMAN AND TOOTSIE
AND AMAZING GRACE AND SHEILA

Soups

Soup Intr

THE MOST IMPORTANT FACTOR IN GOOD SOUPS IS FRESH INGREDIENTS
MEAT. MOST STOCK RECIPES CALL FOR, IN ADDITION TO THESE TWO INGRED
FIND THEM ESSENTIAL. IF THERE HAPPENS TO BE A POT OF STOCK COOKIN
ADDED. HOWEVER, DON'T TREAT STOCK POTS AS GARBAGE PAILS. STRONG
THE GOOD STOCK FLAVOR.

OUR CHICKEN AND BEEF STOCKS ARE COOKED ANYWHERE FROM 8 TO 3
STOCK. USE ABOUT ONE POUND OF CHICKEN BONES PER QUART OF WATE
BEEF BONES WILL DO. AGAIN, THE PROPORTION IS ABOUT ONE POUND C
MEAT FOR EXTRA FLAVOR.

duction

...RESHLY PREPARED. THIS INCLUDES MEAT STOCKS MADE FROM BONES AND
...NTS, ONIONS, CELERY, CARROTS, HERBS, ETC. THESE ARE FINE, BUT WE DON'T
...ND SOME CELERY LEAVES AND PARSLEY STEMS GOING TO WASTE, THEY ARE
...NSISTENT VEGETABLES — CABBAGE, BROCCOLI LEAVES, ETC. — DETRACT FROM

...OURS OVER VERY LOW HEAT. CHICKEN BACKS AND NECKS MAKE FINE CHICKEN
...EEF MARROW AND KNUCKLE BONES MAKE THE BEST STOCK, BUT ANY KIND OF
...ONES PER QUART OF WATER, WITH THE ADDITION OF 1/3 POUND OF SHANK

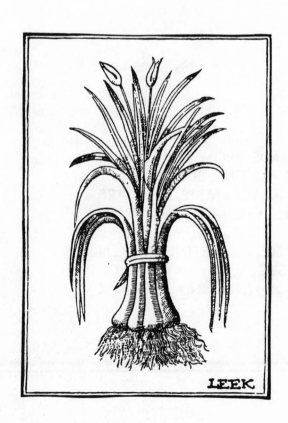

LEEK

Basque Bean Soup

(MAKES 12 CUPS)

1/2 POUND PINTO OR PINK BEANS

WATER

1/4 POUND SLAB OR SLICED BACON

1 CUP CHOPPED ONION

1 CLOVE GARLIC, FINELY CHOPPED

1 CUP CHOPPED CARROT

1 CUP CHOPPED TURNIP

1 CUP DICED GREEN PEPPER

1/4 CUP SLICED LEEK

1-1/2 CUPS DICED POTATOES

3/4 TEASPOON THYME LEAVES

1/2 TEASPOON CRUSHED RED PEPPER

1/4 POUND KIELBASA OR OTHER GARLIC
   SAUSAGE

3 CUPS DRY RED WINE

2-1/2 CUPS SHREDDED CABBAGE

SALT

WASH BEANS AND SOAK OVERNIGHT IN WATER TO COVER. DRAIN. PLACE SLAB BACON IN ONE PIECE IN SOUP POT. IF SLICED BACON IS USED, CHOP BEFORE ADDING. ADD BEANS TO POT ALONG WITH 1-1/2 QUARTS WATER. BRING TO A BOIL, REDUCE HEAT AND SIMMER 2 HOURS. ADD VEGETABLES (RESERVE CABBAGE), HERBS, SAUSAGE (IN ONE PIECE) AND WINE. RETURN TO A BOIL. REDUCE HEAT AND SIMMER 1-1/2 HOURS.

REMOVE BACON, IF IN A SLAB, AND THE SAUSAGE. DICE SAUSAGE; RETURN TO SOUP AND PUT SLAB BACON IN BLENDER WITH SOME OF THE STOCK. BLEND UNTIL SMOOTH AND POUR INTO SOUP. ADD CABBAGE AND CONTINUE COOKING 15 TO 20 MINUTES. SEASON TO TASTE WITH SALT. SERVE SOUP GARNISHED WITH CHOPPED PARSLEY IF DESIRED.

Black Bean Soup

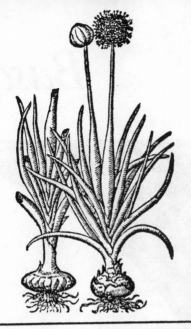

(MAKES 14 CUPS)

2-1/2 CUPS BLACK BEANS
WATER
6 OUNCES SALT PORK
2 CUPS CHOPPED ONION
1 CUP CHOPPED CELERY
1 CUP CHOPPED CARROT
1 CRUMBLED BAY LEAF
3 WHOLE CLOVES

1/2 TEASPOON CRUSHED RED PEPPER
PINCH MACE
1 TABLESPOON VINEGAR
1 CUP MEDIUM SHERRY
SALT TO TASTE
CHOPPED HARD-COOKED EGG OR THIN
     LEMON SLICES

WASH, THEN SOAK BEANS OVERNIGHT IN WATER TO COVER. DRAIN. ADD BEANS TO SOUP POT WITH 3 QUARTS OF WATER AND THE SALT PORK. BRING TO A BOIL AND SKIM OFF FOAM. REDUCE HEAT AND SIMMER TWO HOURS.

ADD CHOPPED VEGETABLES, HERBS AND SPICES. CONTINUE SIMMERING FOR ANOTHER 2 HOURS. PUREE SOUP IN BLENDER, A LITTLE AT A TIME. RETURN TO SOUP POT AND ADD VINEGAR AND SHERRY. SEASON TO TASTE WITH SALT. SERVE GARNISHED WITH HARD-COOKED EGG OR LEMON SLICES.

Cheddar Cheese Soup

(MAKES 10 CUPS)

1/2 CUP DICED BACON (ABOUT 2 OUNCES)

1 TABLESPOON BUTTER

1 CUP CHOPPED CARROT

1 CUP CHOPPED ONION

1 CUP CHOPPED CELERY

3/4 CUP CHOPPED GREEN PEPPER

3 CUPS CHICKEN STOCK

1-1/2 CUPS BEER

3-1/2 CUPS MILK

1 POUND SHARP VERMONT CHEDDAR CHEESE, SHREDDED

2/3 CUP FLOUR

1/2 CUP HEAVY CREAM

SALT AND PEPPER TO TASTE

CHOPPED PARSLEY

SAUTE BACON IN BUTTER UNTIL CRISP AND BROWN. REMOVE BACON WITH SLOTTED SPOON AND DRAIN ON PAPER TOWEL; RESERVE. ADD VEGETABLES TO BACON DRIPPINGS AND COOK, STIRRING OCCASIONALLY, UNTIL ONION IS TRANSPARENT. ADD VEGETABLES TO SOUP POT WITH STOCK AND BEER. HEAT TO BOILING, THEN SIMMER UNTIL VEGETABLES ARE TENDER.

SCALD MILK OVER MEDIUM HEAT. COMBINE CHEESE AND FLOUR IN PLASTIC BAG; TOSS TO COMBINE. WHEN MILK IS HOT, ADD CHEESE-FLOUR MIXTURE. COOK AND STIR UNTIL CHEESE MELTS AND MIXTURE THICKENS. ADD TO SOUP POT WITH CREAM. SEASON TO TASTE WITH SALT AND PEPPER AND HEAT TO SERVING TEMPERATURE. GARNISH WITH RESERVED BACON AND PARSLEY.

Chilled Herb and Tomato Soup

A GOOD HOT WEATHER SOUP, BUT IT REALLY NEEDS TO AGE A DAY OR TWO WITH THE HERBS.

(MAKES 5 CUPS)

1 QUART TOMATO JUICE
(SACRAMENTO IS BEST)

1/4 CUP SALAD OIL

1/4 CUP VINEGAR

1/2 CUP MILK

2 TABLESPOONS LEMON JUICE

1 CLOVE GARLIC, MASHED

2 TABLESPOONS SUGAR

1 TEASPOON DRY MUSTARD

1 TABLESPOON ROSEMARY LEAVES

1 TABLESPOON BASIL LEAVES

1 TEASPOON THYME LEAVES

SALT AND PEPPER TO TASTE

1-1/4 CUPS CHOPPED PEELED CUCUMBER

COMBINE TOMATO JUICE, OIL AND VINEGAR. BEAT IN MILK AND LEMON JUICE. ADD GARLIC, SUGAR AND HERBS. CHILL AT LEAST 24 HOURS. STRAIN OUT HERBS, SEASON TO TASTE WITH SALT AND PEPPER. SERVE SOUP WITH CHOPPED CUCUMBER.

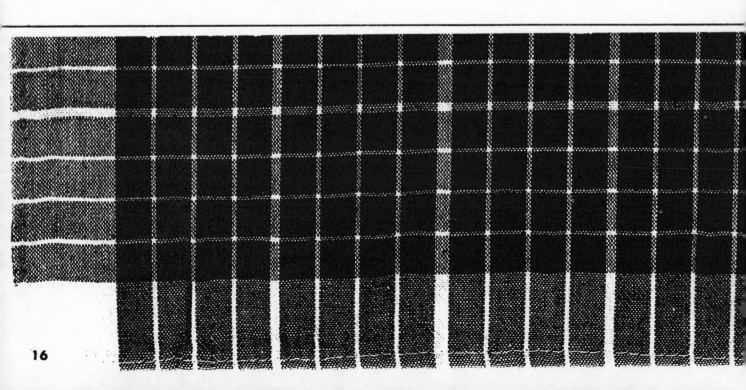

Chlodnik

SAUERKRAUT JUICE IS UNOBTAINABLE IN VERMONT SO WE PUT CANNED SAUERKRAUT AND JUICE WITH A LITTLE WATER THROUGH THE BLENDER AND ADD THE MIXTURE TO THE SOUP.

(MAKES 12 CUPS)

1/2 POUND RAW, CLEANED SHRIMP

2 CUPS PEELED, SEEDED, AND DICED CUCUMBERS (ABOUT 2 MEDIUM)

1 TEASPOON SALT

2 CUPS SOUR CREAM

5 CUPS YOGURT OR BUTTERMILK

1/2 CUP SAUERKRAUT JUICE

2 CLOVES GARLIC, FINELY CHOPPED

1/2 CUP CHOPPED FRESH FENNEL OR 1 TEASPOON GROUND FENNEL SEED

1/2 CUP SLICED SCALLIONS

SALT AND PEPPER TO TASTE

2 HARD-COOKED EGGS, SIEVED

DROP SHRIMP INTO BOILING WATER; BRING TO A BOIL AGAIN AND IMMEDIATELY DRAIN. PLACE SHRIMP IN COLD SALTED WATER AND CHILL. COMBINE CUCUMBER AND SALT, LET STAND 30 MINUTES. DRAIN. CHOP SHRIMP.

COMBINE SOUR CREAM, YOGURT AND KRAUT JUICE IN STAINLESS STEEL OR CERAMIC BOWL; BEAT UNTIL SMOOTH. ADD GARLIC, FENNEL, SCALLIONS, SHRIMP AND CUCUMBER. SEASON TO TASTE WITH SALT AND PEPPER. CHILL VERY WELL. SERVE GARNISHED WITH HARD-COOKED EGGS.

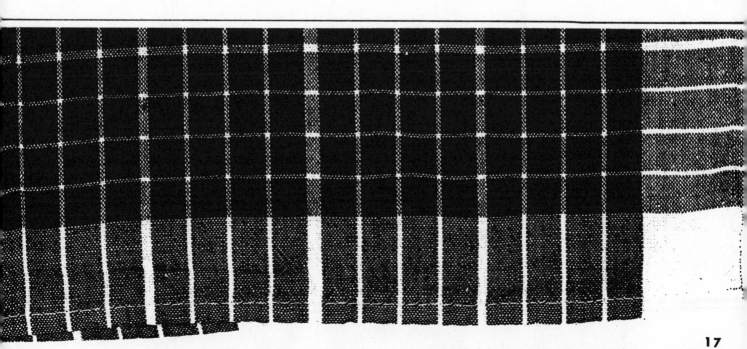

Corn Chowder

(MAKES 10 CUPS)

2 OUNCES (1/2 CUP) DICED SALT PORK
   OR BACON

2 TABLESPOONS BUTTER

3/4 CUP CHOPPED ONION

3/4 CUP CHOPPED CELERY

1 QUART CHICKEN STOCK

2 CUPS DICED POTATOES

6 CUPS FRESH CORN KERNELS OR
   3 PACKAGES (10 OUNCES EACH) FROZEN
   KERNEL CORN, THAWED

1 CUP HEAVY CREAM

SALT AND PEPPER TO TASTE

CHOPPED PARSLEY

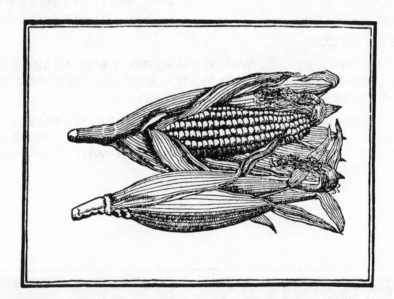

SAUTE SALT PORK IN BUTTER UNTIL CRISP AND BROWNED. ADD ONION AND CELERY. COOK UNTIL VEGETABLES ARE CRISP-TENDER. MEANWHILE, MEASURE STOCK IN SOUP POT; ADD POTATOES AND COOK UNTIL JUST TENDER.

PUREE 2 PACKAGES OF CORN IN BLENDER, USING A LITTLE OF THE HOT STOCK WHILE BLENDING. ADD BLENDED CORN AND WHOLE KERNELS, SAUTEED VEGETABLES AND CREAM TO SOUP POT. SEASON TO TASTE WITH SALT AND PEPPER. HEAT TO SERVING TEMPERATURE. SERVE WITH PARSLEY GARNISH.

French Fish Stew

THIS IS A VARIATION ON BOUILLABAISSE BUT WITHOUT ITS GREATER VARIETY OF FISH AND SHELLFISH.

(MAKES 12 CUPS)

1/4 CUP OLIVE OIL

1/2 CUP CHOPPED ONION

1/3 CUP SLICED LEEK

2 UNPEELED CLOVES GARLIC, MASHED

1 CAN (28 OUNCES) WHOLE TOMATOES

1-1/2 QUARTS WATER

3 SPRIGS PARSLEY

1 BAY LEAF

1/4 TEASPOON THYME

1/8 TEASPOON FENNEL SEED

1 PINCH SAFFRON

2-INCH PIECE ORANGE PEEL

1/8 TEASPOON PEPPER

2 TEASPOONS SALT

2 POUNDS FISH SCRAPS (HEADS, TAILS AND BONES)

1 POUND FISH FILLET, CUT UP

1 POUND BLUE SHELL MUSSELS

DRY BREAD ROUNDS

CHOPPED PARSLEY AND ROUILLE

HEAT OIL IN SOUP POT. ADD ONION, LEEK AND GARLIC. SAUTE UNTIL ALMOST TENDER. DRAIN TOMATOES AND CUT IN QUARTERS, REMOVING AS MANY SEEDS AS POSSIBLE. ADD HALF THE TOMATOES AND ALL THE JUICE TO THE SAUTEED ONIONS. RESERVE REMAINING TOMATOES. HEAT INGREDIENTS IN SOUP POT TO A BOIL; SIMMER 5 MINUTES. ADD WATER, SEASONINGS AND FISH SCRAPS. BRING TO A BOIL AND SIMMER ABOUT 1 HOUR.

STRAIN SOUP STOCK THROUGH COLANDER, PRESSING LIQUID OUT OF SOLIDS. DISCARD SOLIDS AND BRING STOCK TO A BOIL. ADD RESERVED TOMATOES, THE FISH FILLETS AND MUSSELS. BRING TO A BOIL AND SERVE IMMEDIATELY, POURING SOUP OVER DRY BREAD ROUNDS. GARNISH WITH CHOPPED PARSLEY AND PASS A BOWL OF ROUILLE.

ROUILLE

(MAKES 1 CUP)

1 OR 2 DRIED HOT CHILI PEPPERS

1 MEDIUM POTATO, DICED

1/2 CUP FISH STOCK

1/4 CUP CHOPPED PIMIENTO

4 CLOVES GARLIC

1 TEASPOON BASIL LEAVES

1/3 CUP OLIVE OIL

COOK CHILI PEPPERS AND POTATO IN FISH STOCK UNTIL TENDER. POUR INTO BLENDER JAR WITH PIMIENTO, GARLIC AND BASIL. BLEND UNTIL SMOOTH, THEN REMOVE BLENDER COVER. GRADUALLY ADD OLIVE OIL WHILE MIXTURE CONTINUES TO BLEND. SERVE WITH FRENCH FISH STEW.

Fresh Tomato Bisque

(MAKES 9 CUPS)

1-1/2 QUARTS CUT UP, FRESH, RIPE TOMATOES (ABOUT 3 POUNDS)

1/3 CUP BUTTER

2 CUPS DRY BREAD CUBES

1-1/2 TEASPOONS SALT

1/4 TEASPOON FRESHLY GROUND PEPPER

3 CLOVES GARLIC

6 CUPS WATER

1-1/2 CUPS HEAVY CREAM

2 EGG YOLKS

BUTTERED CROUTONS

CUT UP AND MEASURE TOMATOES (DO NOT PEEL OR SEED). HEAT BUTTER IN SOUP POT. ADD TOMATOES AND COVER. SIMMER 5 MINUTES. ADD DRY BREAD CUBES, SALT AND PEPPER. MASH UNPEELED GARLIC WITH SIDE OF KNIFE AND ADD TO TOMATOES WITH WATER. BRING TO A BOIL. COVER AND SIMMER 1 HOUR. SIEVE SOUP AND RETURN TO SOUP POT. SIMMER FOR ANOTHER HOUR.

GRADUALLY BEAT CREAM INTO EGG YOLKS. ADD CREAM MIXTURE TO TOMATO STOCK, BEATING CONSTANTLY. HEAT TO SERVING TEMPERATURE BUT DO NOT BOIL. SERVE WITH CROUTONS.

Indian Mulligatawney

(MAKES 9 CUPS)

1 TABLESPOON OIL
2 TABLESPOONS BUTTER
3/4 CUP CHOPPED ONION
3/4 CUP CHOPPED CARROT
3/4 CUP CHOPPED CELERY
2/3 CUP CHOPPED GREEN PEPPER
1/2 CUP CHOPPED TURNIP
3/4 CUP CHOPPED APPLE
2 TEASPOONS SALT

1/2 TEASPOON CRUSHED RED PEPPER
1-1/2 TEASPOONS CURRY POWDER
6 CUPS CHICKEN STOCK
1 TABLESPOON CORNSTARCH
1/4 CUP COLD WATER
1/4 CUP TOMATO PASTE
2 CUPS DICED COOKED CHICKEN
1-1/2 CUPS PUREED GARBANZO BEANS*
CHOPPED PARSLEY

HEAT OIL AND BUTTER IN SAUCEPAN. ADD CHOPPED VEGETABLES AND APPLES, SALT, RED PEPPER AND CURRY POWDER. COOK, STIRRING FREQUENTLY, UNTIL ONIONS ARE ALMOST TENDER.

MEANWHILE, HEAT STOCK TO BOILING POINT. MAKE A SMOOTH PASTE OF CORNSTARCH AND WATER. ADD TO STOCK, STIRRING CONSTANTLY, UNTIL STOCK RETURNS TO BOIL. ADD SAUTEED VEGETABLES AND REMAINING INGREDIENTS, EXCEPT PARSLEY. HEAT TO SERVING TEMPERATURE. SERVE GARNISHED WITH CHOPPED PARSLEY.

* CANNED OR COOKED DRIED GARBANZOS MAY BE USED. IF USING DRIED, SOAK 1/2 CUP DRIED BEANS OVERNIGHT IN COLD WATER. COOK SOAKED BEANS UNTIL TENDER, THEN BLEND IN BLENDER UNTIL VERY SMOOTH.

Italian Meatball Soup

(MAKES 10 CUPS)

6 CUPS BEEF STOCK

1-1/2 TEASPOONS SALT

2 TABLESPOONS TOMATO PASTE

TIED IN A CHEESECLOTH:

   3 SPRIGS PARSLEY

   1 BAY LEAF

   6 PEPPERCORNS

3/4 CUP CHOPPED ONION

3/4 CUP CHOPPED CARROT

3/4 CUP CHOPPED CELERY

1 CUP DICED POTATO

1 TEASPOON BASIL LEAVES

25 ITALIAN MEATBALLS

1/2 POUND ESCAROLE, CHOPPED

GRATED PARMESAN CHEESE

COMBINE STOCK, SALT, TOMATO PASTE AND HERBS TIED IN CHEESECLOTH. BR
TO A BOIL AND SIMMER 30 MINUTES. ADD CHOPPED VEGETABLES AND BASIL; SIMME
MINUTES LONGER. REMOVE HERB BAG.

ADD MEATBALLS AND ESCAROLE. BRING TO A BOIL AND SIMMER 10 MINUTES. SE
WITH PARMESAN CHEESE.

ITALIAN MEATBALLS

(MAKES ABOUT 25)

1/2 POUND LEAN GROUND BEEF

1 EGG

1 CLOVE GARLIC, MINCED

3 TABLESPOONS MINCED PARSLEY

1/2 TEASPOON SALT

1/4 TEASPOON PEPPER

1/4 TEASPOON OREGANO

1 TEASPOON LEMON JUICE

3 TABLESPOONS GRATED PARMESAN
CHEESE

COMBINE ALL INGREDIENTS AND MIX VERY WELL. CHILL 1 TO 2 HOURS, THEN SH
INTO SMALL BALLS. CHILL ABOUT 30 MINUTES BEFORE ADDING TO SOUP. MEATBALLS M
BE PRE-COOKED IN BEEF STOCK, THEN FROZEN.

Joan's Peoria Chili

(MAKES 16 CUPS)

2 TABLESPOONS OIL

2 CUPS CHOPPED ONION

1 TEASPOON CHOPPED GARLIC

1 CUP CHOPPED GREEN PEPPER

2 POUNDS GROUND BEEF

4 CANS (1 POUND EACH) CANNED TOMATOES

1 CAN (12 OUNCES) TOMATO PASTE

4 CANS (1 POUND EACH) CANNED KIDNEY BEANS

2 CUPS WATER

1-1/2 TABLESPOONS SALT

1/2 TEASPOON CRUSHED RED PEPPER

3-4 TABLESPOONS CHILI POWDER (MORE OR LESS TO TASTE)

HEAT OIL IN SOUP POT. ADD ONION, GARLIC AND GREEN PEPPER. SAUTE UNTIL CRISP-TENDER. REMOVE SAUTEED VEGETABLES WITH SLOTTED SPOON. ADD GROUND BEEF AND COOK UNTIL WELL BROWNED. STIR FREQUENTLY AND BREAK UP MEAT AS IT BROWNS. ADD ADDITIONAL OIL, IF NECESSARY.

ADD SAUTEED VEGETABLES TO BROWNED MEAT ALONG WITH REMAINING INGREDIENTS. BRING TO A BOIL. REDUCE HEAT AND SIMMER OVER LOW HEAT 3 TO 4 HOURS. STIR FREQUENTLY TO PREVENT BURNING. TASTE AFTER 2 HOURS AND SEASON WITH ADDITIONAL CHILI, SALT AND PEPPER TO TASTE.

Kidney Bean Soup

  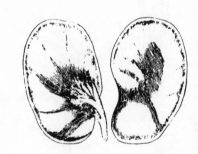

(MAKES 15 CUPS)

1 POUND DRY RED KIDNEY BEANS

4 QUARTS COLD WATER

1 TABLESPOON SALT

1 TEASPOON PEPPER

1 BAY LEAF

1/2 CUP OIL

3 CUPS CHOPPED ONIONS

1-1/2 TEASPOONS CHOPPED GARLIC

2 CUPS MILK

2 TABLESPOONS WINE VINEGAR

SOUR CREAM

WASH BEANS THOROUGHLY. SOAK OVERNIGHT IN COLD WATER IN SOUP POT. ADD SALT, PEPPER AND BAY LEAF. BRING TO A BOIL. REDUCE HEAT AND SIMMER 2 HOURS. ADD ADDITIONAL WATER TO KEEP LIQUID UP TO LEVEL. REMOVE BAY LEAF AND PUREE BEANS IN BLENDER. RETURN TO SOUP POT.

MEANWHILE, HEAT OIL IN SKILLET. ADD ONIONS AND GARLIC. SAUTE OVER LOW HEAT UNTIL ONIONS ARE TENDER. ADD ONIONS WITH OIL, THE MILK AND VINEGAR TO PUREED BEANS. HEAT TO SERVING TEMPERATURE, STIRRING OCCASIONALLY. SERVE GARNISHED WITH SOUR CREAM.

Lamb and Barley Soup

(MAKES 16 CUPS)

4 POUNDS BONE-IN LAMB STEW MEAT

4 QUARTS WATER

10 WHOLE CLOVES

2 MEDIUM ONIONS, HALVED

4 CELERY STALKS, HALVED

2 BAY LEAVES

2 TABLESPOONS SALT

1/4 TEASPOON PEPPER

2/3 CUP PEARL BARLEY

3/4 CUP CHOPPED PARSNIPS

1 CUP SHREDDED CARROT

1/2 CUP SLICED LEEK

CHOPPED PARSLEY

COMBINE LAMB AND WATER IN SOUP POT. BRING TO A BOIL AND SKIM OFF FOAM. SIMMER 40 MINUTES, OR UNTIL MEAT IS JUST BARELY TENDER. REMOVE MEAT AND BONES AND SET ASIDE TO COOL.

STICK WHOLE CLOVES INTO ONIONS. ADD ONIONS, CELERY, BAY LEAVES, SALT AND PEPPER TO LAMB STOCK. BRING TO A BOIL; REDUCE HEAT AND SIMMER 3 TO 4 HOURS.

REMOVE MEAT AND FAT FROM BONES. DISCARD FAT AND RETURN BONES TO SIMMERING STOCK. CUT MEAT INTO SMALL PIECES AND RESERVE.

STRAIN BONES AND VEGETABLES FROM STOCK. RETURN STOCK TO SOUP POT AND DISCARD BONES AND VEGETABLES. SKIM OFF ALL FAT FROM STOCK. (IF CHILLED OVERNIGHT, SOLID FAT MAY BE EASILY REMOVED FROM TOP OF STOCK.)

HEAT STOCK TO A BOIL AND ADD BARLEY. SIMMER 40 TO 50 MINUTES. ADD PARSNIP, CARROT, LEEK AND RESERVED LAMB; SIMMER 10 TO 15 MINUTES. SERVE GARNISHED WITH PARSLEY.

Lentil Soup

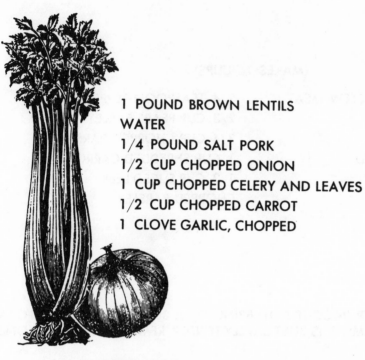

1 POUND BROWN LENTILS
WATER
1/4 POUND SALT PORK
1/2 CUP CHOPPED ONION
1 CUP CHOPPED CELERY AND LEAVES
1/2 CUP CHOPPED CARROT
1 CLOVE GARLIC, CHOPPED

1 BAY LEAF, CRUMBLED
1 TEASPOON SUGAR
1/4 TEASPOON THYME LEAVES
2 TABLESPOONS BUTTER
2 TABLESPOONS FLOUR
1 TABLESPOON LEMON JUICE
THINLY SLICED SCALLIONS

(MAKES 12 CUPS)

WASH LENTILS. SOAK OVERNIGHT IN WATER TO COVER. DRAIN SOAKING WATER AND MEASURE. ADD ADDITIONAL WATER TO MAKE 2-1/2 QUARTS. COMBINE LENTILS, MEASURED WATER AND SALT PORK IN SOUP POT. BRING TO A BOIL. REDUCE HEAT AND SIMMER 2-1/2 HOURS. ADD CHOPPED VEGETABLES, GARLIC, BAY LEAF, SUGAR AND THYME. SIMMER ANOTHER 1 TO 1-1/2 HOURS.

REMOVE SALT PORK FROM SOUP POT AND PUT IN BLENDER JAR WITH A CUP OF SOUP LIQUID. BLEND UNTIL SMOOTH. RETURN TO SOUP POT.

HEAT BUTTER AND BLEND IN FLOUR. ADD 2 CUPS OF HOT SOUP TO FLOUR MIXTURE AND BRING TO A BOIL, STIRRING CONSTANTLY. RETURN TO SOUP AND STIR IN LEMON JUICE. HEAT TO SERVING TEMPERATURE AND SEASON TO TASTE WITH SALT AND PEPPER. SERVE GARNISHED WITH SLICED SCALLIONS.

LUIS DE SOTO IS A SPANISH GENTLEMAN AND A SUPERB COOK. THIS IS HIS RECIPE. THERE IS NO BETTER WAY TO USE GOOD FRESH RIPE TOMATOES.

1/4 POUND DAY-OLD FRENCH BREAD, CUBED

WATER

1-1/2 CUPS DICED, PARED CUCUMBER

1 GREEN PEPPER, SEEDED AND DICED

1 TO 2 CLOVES GARLIC

2 TEASPOONS SALT

1/2 CUP OLIVE OIL

1/4 CUP WINE VINEGAR

2 POUNDS RIPE TOMATOES, SEEDED AND CUBED

GARNISH: CHOPPED CUCUMBER, CROUTONS (FRIED IN OLIVE OIL), CHOPPED CRISP BACON, SLICED PIMIENTO-STUFFED OLIVES.

Luis de Soto's Gazpacho

(MAKES 7 CUPS)

SOAK BREAD IN COLD WATER, TURNING ONCE. SQUEEZE OUT EXCESS WATER. COMBINE CUCUMBER, GREEN PEPPER, GARLIC, SALT, OIL AND VINEGAR IN BLENDER JAR. BLEND UNTIL SMOOTH. ADD HALF THE SOAKED BREAD AND CONTINUE BLENDING UNTIL SMOOTH. POUR INTO REFRIGERATOR CONTAINER (PLASTIC, GLASS, OR STAINLESS STEEL).

ADD TOMATOES TO BLENDER JAR WITH REMAINING BREAD; BLEND UNTIL SMOOTH AND ADD TO REFRIGERATOR CONTAINER. ADD ADDITIONAL SALT AND VINEGAR TO TASTE. CHILL SEVERAL HOURS OR OVERNIGHT. SERVE WITH GARNISHES.

(MAKES 11 CUPS)

3 POUNDS SMOKED HAM HOCKS

3-1/2 QUARTS WATER

1 POUND GREEN SPLIT PEAS

1-1/4 CUPS CHOPPED ONION

1-1/4 CUPS CHOPPED CARROT

1-1/2 CUPS DICED HAM (CUT FROM HAM HOCKS)

1 TABLESPOON SALT

1/4 TEASPOON PEPPER

CROUTONS

COMBINE HAM HOCKS AND WATER IN SOUP POT. BRING TO A BOIL. REDUCE HEAT AND SIMMER 2 TO 3 HOURS. REMOVE HAM HOCKS AND SET ASIDE TO COOL.

SKIM OFF EXCESS FAT FROM HAM STOCK. WASH SPLIT PEAS AND ADD TO STOCK. BRING TO A BOIL AND SIMMER 2 HOURS. ADD CHOPPED ONION AND CARROT. SIMMER FOR 1 HOUR.

MEANWHILE, REMOVE MEAT FROM HAM HOCKS, DICE AND MEASURE. ADD DICED HAM, SALT AND PEPPER TO SOUP. HEAT TO SERVING TEMPERATURE AND SERVE WITH CROUTONS.

Marge Warder's Pea Soup

IF YOU CAN FIND IT, USE PROSCIUTTO HAM — FINELY CHOPPED AND USE ABOUT HALF AS MUCH AS INDICATED IN THIS RECIPE.

(MAKES ABOUT 24 CUPS)

1/2 POUND GREAT NORTHERN BEANS
WATER
1/4 CUP OLIVE OIL
1/4 CUP BUTTER OR MARGARINE
1-1/4 CUPS CHOPPED CARROT
2-1/2 CUPS CHOPPED CELERY
1-1/2 CUPS CHOPPED ONION
1 CAN (16 OUNCES) TOMATOES
4 QUARTS BEEF OR CHICKEN STOCK
2 CUPS DICED POTATOES
1-1/2 TABLESPOONS SALT

1 CLOVE GARLIC, CRUSHED
1/4 CUP ROUGH-CUT PARSLEY
1 TABLESPOON BASIL LEAVES
1/2 TEASPOON OREGANO
1/2 POUND DICED COOKED HAM
1 PACKAGE (9 OUNCES) FROZEN
   ITALIAN GREEN BEANS
1 POUND ZUCCHINI, SLICED
1/2 CUP ELBOW MACARONI
2 CUPS SHREDDED CABBAGE
GRATED PARMESAN CHEESE

WASH AND SOAK BEANS OVERNIGHT IN COLD WATER. DRAIN AND COOK IN WATER TO COVER UNTIL NOT QUITE TENDER. DRAIN AND SET ASIDE.

HEAT OIL AND BUTTER IN SAUCEPAN. ADD CARROT, CELERY AND ONION; SAUTE 5 MINUTES. ADD TOMATOES AND BRING TO A BOIL. BREAK UP TOMATOES AND SIMMER 10 TO 15 MINUTES.

MEANWHILE, COMBINE STOCK AND POTATOES IN SOUP POT. BRING TO A BOIL AND COOK UNTIL POTATOES ARE JUST TENDER. ADD THE SIMMERING VEGETABLES, THE RE-SERVED BEANS, SEASONINGS, HAM AND ITALIAN GREEN BEANS. BRING TO A BOIL AND SIMMER 20 MINUTES. ADD ZUCCHINI, MACARONI AND CABBAGE. SIMMER 15 MINUTES. SERVE GARNISHED WITH GRATED PARMESAN CHEESE.

Minestrone

New England Clam Chowder

(MAKES 16 CUPS)

3 DOZEN LARGE CHERRYSTONE CLAMS

1-1/4 QUARTS DICED POTATOES

2 QUARTS MILK

1/4 CUP FLOUR

4 OUNCES SALT PORK, DICED (ABOUT 1 CUP)

1 TABLESPOON BUTTER

1-1/2 CUPS CHOPPED ONION

1 CUP LIGHT CREAM

1/4 TEASPOON THYME

1/8 TEASPOON PEPPER

SALT TO TASTE

CHOPPED PARSLEY

SHUCK CLAMS* CAREFULLY, CATCHING JUICE AS CLAMS ARE OPENED. WASH CLAMS IN JUICE AND LIFT OUT CLAMS. STRAIN JUICE THROUGH TRIPLE THICKNESS OF CHEESE-CLOTH AND ADD WATER IF NECESSARY TO MAKE 4-1/2 CUPS. PLACE IN SOUP POT WITH POTATOES. BRING TO A BOIL, THEN SIMMER UNTIL POTATOES ARE TENDER. COMBINE 1 CUP OF THE MILK AND THE FLOUR; BLEND UNTIL SMOOTH. POUR INTO BOILING CLAM MIX-TURE, STIRRING CONSTANTLY UNTIL MIXTURE RETURNS TO A BOIL. SET ASIDE.

CUT AWAY TOUGH MUSCLE FROM CLAMS AND GRIND OR BLEND MUSCLE IN BLENDER. COARSELY CHOP THE REST OF THE CLAMS. ADD GROUND (OR BLENDED) AND CHOPPED CLAMS TO COOKED POTATOES.

MEANWHILE, COOK SALT PORK IN WATER TO COVER FOR 10 MINUTES. DRAIN AND DRY ON PAPER TOWELS. HEAT BUTTER IN SKILLET AND ADD SALT PORK. COOK, STIRRING FREQUENTLY, UNTIL PORK IS CRISP AND BROWN. REMOVE AND DRAIN ON PAPER TOWEL. ADD ONION TO PORK DRIPPINGS; SAUTE UNTIL TENDER.

ADD ONIONS, REMAINING MILK, CREAM, SALT PORK AND SEASONINGS TO CLAM AND POTATO MIXTURE. HEAT TO SERVING TEMPERATURE, STIRRING FREQUENTLY. LET STAND AT ROOM TEMPERATURE FOR 1 HOUR. TASTE AND SEASON WITH SALT, IF NECES-SARY. REHEAT TO SERVING TEMPERATURE. SERVE WITH CHOPPED PARSLEY.

* CLAMS MAY BE STEAMED OPEN IN A LITTLE WATER BEFORE SHUCKING. USE STEAMING WATER AS PART OF CLAM JUICE.

Peasant Cabbage Soup

THIS IS MUCH LIKE A NEW ENGLAND BOILED DINNER.

(MAKES 24 CUPS)

HAM BONE
4 QUARTS WATER
1 QUART DICED BOILING POTATOES
3 QUARTS COARSELY CHOPPED CABBAGE
2 MEDIUM ONIONS, CHOPPED
2 LARGE CARROTS, CHOPPED
2 CUPS DICED TURNIPS
3 RIBS CELERY, SLICED
1/3 POUND KIELBASA OR OTHER GARLIC SAUSAGE
2 CUPS PARTIALLY COOKED PEA BEANS

TIED IN CHEESECLOTH:
 6 PARSLEY SPRIGS
 1/2 TEASPOON MARJORAM
 1/2 TEASPOON THYME LEAVES
 4 CLOVES GARLIC, MASHED
 2 WHOLE CLOVES
 10 PEPPERCORNS, CRUSHED
1-1/2 POUNDS HAM, DICED
SALT TO TASTE
CHOPPED PARSLEY

COMBINE HAM BONE AND WATER IN SOUP POT. BRING TO A BOIL AND SIMMER 2 HOURS. ADD WATER TO KEEP LIQUID UP TO LEVEL. REMOVE AND DISCARD BONE. ADD ALL CHOPPED VEGETABLES, KIELBASA, PEA BEANS AND HERB BAG. BRING TO A BOIL AND SIMMER 2-1/2 TO 3 HOURS. REMOVE HERB BAG AND KIELBASA. DISCARD HERBS AND DICE SAUSAGE. ADD SAUSAGE TO SOUP WITH HAM. SEASON TO TASTE WITH SALT. SIMMER 20 MINUTES. GARNISH WITH CHOPPED PARSLEY AND SERVE WITH DIJON MUSTARD, IF DESIRED.

Onion Soup au Gratin

A RICH BEEF STOCK, SLOWLY BROWNED ONIONS AND GOOD CHEESE MAKE THIS SOUP.

(MAKES 9 CUPS)

1-1/2 POUNDS YELLOW ONIONS, THINLY SLICED
3 TABLESPOONS BUTTER
1 TABLESPOON OIL
1 TEASPOON SALT
1 TEASPOON SUGAR
3 TABLESPOONS FLOUR

2 QUARTS BOILING BEEF STOCK
1/2 CUP DRY VERMOUTH
SALT AND PEPPER TO TASTE
2 TABLESPOONS COGNAC
DRY BREAD ROUNDS
1-1/4 CUPS GRATED SWISS CHEESE
1/3 CUP GRATED PARMESAN CHEESE

COMBINE ONIONS, BUTTER AND OIL IN HEAVY SKILLET. COVER AND SIMMER OVER LOW HEAT 15 TO 20 MINUTES, OR UNTIL ONIONS WILT. UNCOVER AND RAISE HEAT TO MEDIUM. SPRINKLE WITH SALT AND SUGAR. SAUTE, STIRRING FREQUENTLY, ABOUT 45 MINUTES, OR UNTIL ONIONS ARE A DEEP GOLDEN BROWN.

SPRINKLE FLOUR OVER ONIONS AND CONTINUE COOKING, STIRRING CONSTANTLY, 2 TO 3 MINUTES. REMOVE FROM HEAT AND STIR IN BOILING STOCK. STIR UNTIL SOUP BOILS, THEN ADD VERMOUTH AND SALT AND PEPPER TO TASTE. SIMMER OVER VERY LOW HEAT 30 MINUTES. STIR IN COGNAC. LADLE INTO SOUP BOWLS OVER BREAD ROUNDS AND TOP WITH A MIXTURE OF CHEESES. SERVE AT ONCE.

Oyster Stew

(MAKES 6 CUPS)

2 TABLESPOONS BUTTER
2 CUPS RAW OYSTERS IN THEIR JUICE
DASH WORCESTERSHIRE

2 CUPS MILK
2 CUPS LIGHT CREAM
SALT AND PEPPER TO TASTE

HEAT BUTTER IN LARGE SAUCEPAN. ADD OYSTERS AND STIR OVER MEDIUM HEAT UNTIL EDGES START TO CURL. LIFT OUT OYSTERS WITH SLOTTED SPOON.

ADD WORCESTERSHIRE, MILK AND CREAM TO OYSTER JUICE. HEAT TO SERVING TEMPERATURE. ADD OYSTERS AND SEASON TO TASTE WITH SALT AND PEPPER.

SERVE GARNISHED WITH ADDITIONAL BUTTER, IF DESIRED.

Parsley Soup

(MAKES 12 CUPS)

1 QUART DICED POTATOES

1 CUP DICED ONION

1/4 CUP BUTTER

1/4 TEASPOON CURRY POWDER

1 TEASPOON WORCESTERSHIRE

1-1/4 CUPS WATER

2 CUPS PARSLEY SPRIGS THAT HAVE HAD
   ALL STEMS REMOVED

3 CUPS CHICKEN STOCK

3 CUPS MILK

2 TEASPOONS SALT

1 CUP HEAVY CREAM

1/4 TEASPOON PEPPER

COMBINE POTATOES, ONION, BUTTER, CURRY POWDER, WORCESTERSHIRE AND WATER IN SAUCEPAN. BRING TO A BOIL AND SIMMER UNTIL POTATOES AND ONIONS ARE VERY TENDER.

MEANWHILE, PUT PARSLEY AND CHICKEN STOCK IN BLENDER JAR. BLEND UNTIL VERY SMOOTH. BLEND POTATO MIXTURE WITH SOME OF THE MILK UNTIL SMOOTH. COMBINE PARSLEY AND POTATO MIXTURE IN SOUP POT WITH ANY REMAINING MILK, THE SALT, CREAM AND PEPPER. SEASON WITH ADDITIONAL SALT TO TASTE. HEAT TO SERVING TEMPERATURE, OR CHILL AND SERVE VERY COLD.

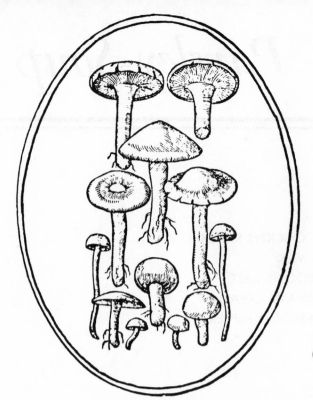

(MAKES 18 CUPS)

3 CUPS DRIED MUSHROOMS (ABOUT
    1-1/2 OUNCES)
1-1/2 QUARTS WATER
1/2 CUP BUTTER
1-1/2 CUPS CHOPPED ONION
3-1/2 CUPS CHOPPED CELERY
2 TEASPOONS CARAWAY SEED

1-1/2 QUARTS DICED POTATOES
1/2 CUP FLOUR
2 QUARTS MILK
1 CUP HEAVY CREAM
SALT AND PEPPER TO TASTE
CHOPPED CHIVES OR PARSLEY

COMBINE MUSHROOMS AND WATER IN SAUCEPAN. BRING TO A BOIL AND SIMMER 10 TO 40 MINUTES, OR UNTIL TENDER. TIME DEPENDS UPON TYPE OF MUSHROOM. DRAIN MUSHROOMS AND RESERVE LIQUID. CHOP MUSHROOMS, IF WHOLE.

HEAT BUTTER IN SAME SAUCEPAN. ADD ONION, CELERY, CARAWAY SEED AND MUSHROOMS. SAUTE UNTIL CELERY IS ALMOST TENDER.

MEANWHILE, COMBINE MUSHROOM LIQUID AND POTATOES IN SOUP POT. BRING TO A BOIL. COOK UNTIL POTATOES ARE ALMOST TENDER. ADD SAUTEED VEGETABLES AND RETURN TO BOIL. MASH ABOUT HALF OF THE POTATOES AGAINST THE SIDE OF THE POT WITH A SPOON.

COMBINE FLOUR AND 1 CUP OF THE MILK; BLEND UNTIL SMOOTH. STIR INTO BOIL-ING POTATO MIXTURE; BOIL 2 TO 3 MINUTES. ADD REMAINING MILK AND THE CREAM. SEASON TO TASTE WITH SALT AND PEPPER AND HEAT TO SERVING TEMPERATURE. SERVE GARNISHED WITH CHIVES OR PARSLEY.

Polish Mushroom and Potato Sou

Portuguese Vegetable Soup

(MAKES ABOUT 10 CUPS)

1/2 POUND KIELBASA OR OTHER GARLIC SAUSAGE

WATER

1-1/2 TABLESPOONS OLIVE OIL

1/2 CUP CHOPPED ONION

1 SMALL CLOVE GARLIC, MINCED

2-1/2 CUPS DICED POTATOES

5 CUPS CHICKEN STOCK

1-1/2 CUPS CHOPPED, SEEDED, CANNED OR FRESH TOMATOES*

1/2 CUP DRAINED CANNED KIDNEY BEANS

1/4 POUND CHOPPED KALE, BEET GREENS OR ESCAROLE

SALT AND PEPPER TO TASTE

COVER KIELBASA WITH WATER IN A SKILLET. BRING TO A BOIL AND COOK UNTIL WATER EVAPORATES. REMOVE SAUSAGE AND COOL. CHOP.

ADD OIL, ONIONS AND GARLIC TO SKILLET AND SAUTE UNTIL ONION IS TENDER BUT NOT BROWNED. ADD TO SOUP POT ALONG WITH POTATOES AND STOCK. BRING TO A BOIL AND SIMMER UNTIL POTATOES ARE QUITE TENDER.

STRAIN POTATOES FROM STOCK AND MASH. RETURN TO STOCK WITH TOMATOES, BEANS AND SAUSAGE. SIMMER 5 TO 10 MINUTES. THEN ADD KALE OR BEET GREENS. SIMMER ANOTHER 10 MINUTES. SEASON TO TASTE WITH SALT AND PEPPER. SERVE GARNISHED WITH CHOPPED PARSLEY.

* IF FRESH TOMATOES ARE USED, PEEL BEFORE SEEDING AND CHOPPING.

Potage Bonne Femme

(MAKES 16 CUPS)

2 TABLESPOONS BUTTER
1 CUP SLICED LEEK
3 CUPS CHOPPED ONION
5 CUPS DICED POTATOES
2 QUARTS BOILING WATER
1 POUND SHREDDED CABBAGE

1 CLOVE GARLIC, MINCED
2-1/2 CUPS LIGHT CREAM
3/4 CUP CHOPPED PARSLEY
SALT AND PEPPER TO TASTE
PARSLEY BUTTER

HEAT BUTTER IN SOUP POT. ADD LEEK, ONION, AND POTATOES. SAUTE ABOUT 5 MINUTES, STIRRING FREQUENTLY. ADD BOILING WATER. BRING TO A BOIL AND SIMMER GENTLY 30 MINUTES. ADD CABBAGE AND GARLIC TO SIMMERING MIXTURE. RETURN TO BOIL AND SIMMER 20 MINUTES. ADD CREAM AND PARSLEY AND HEAT TO SERVING TEMPERATURE. SEASON TO TASTE WITH SALT AND PEPPER. SERVE GARNISHED WITH PARSLEY BUTTER.

PARSLEY BUTTER

WHIP 1/2 CUP BUTTER UNTIL LIGHT AND FLUFFY. ADD 2 TABLESPOONS CHOPPED PARSLEY.

Proper Bostonian Bean Soup

(MAKES 12 CUPS)

2 POUNDS SMOKED HAM HOCKS
4 TO 5 QUARTS WATER
1-1/2 POUNDS DRY PEA BEANS
1 LARGE ONION
3 WHOLE CLOVES
1 BAY LEAF

2 TEASPOONS SALT
1-1/2 CUPS CHOPPED ONION
1 CUP CHOPPED CELERY
1 TEASPOON CHOPPED GARLIC
1/2 TEASPOON PEPPER
CHOPPED PARSLEY

COMBINE HAM HOCKS AND 4 QUARTS WATER. BRING TO A BOIL AND SIMMER 3 TO 4 HOURS. REMOVE HAM HOCKS AND SET ASIDE TO COOL. SKIM OFF EXCESS FAT FROM STOCK. ADD BEANS, WHOLE ONION STUCK WITH CLOVES, BAY LEAF AND SALT TO STOCK. BRING TO A BOIL AND SIMMER 2 HOURS. REMOVE ONION AND BAY LEAF. ADD CHOPPED ONION, CELERY, GARLIC AND PEPPER. CONTINUE COOKING ABOUT 1-1/2 HOURS.

MEANWHILE, REMOVE MEAT FROM HOCKS; DICE AND ADD TO SOUP. (HAM SHOULD MEASURE 1-1/2 TO 2 CUPS.) ADD ADDITIONAL WATER IF NECESSARY, AND SALT TO TASTE. SERVE GARNISHED WITH CHOPPED PARSLEY.

Shaker Chicken and Noodle Soup

(MAKES 15 CUPS)

13 CUPS CHICKEN STOCK

1/4 CUP DRY VERMOUTH

1/4 CUP BUTTER

1 CUP HEAVY CREAM

1/2 POUND MEDIUM EGG NOODLES
(ABOUT 4 CUPS)

3/4 CUP FLOUR

1-1/4 CUPS WATER

2 CUPS DICED COOKED CHICKEN

SALT AND PEPPER TO TASTE

CHOPPED PARSLEY

COMBINE 1 CUP OF THE STOCK, THE VERMOUTH AND BUTTER. BRING TO A BOIL AND BOIL RAPIDLY UNTIL MIXTURE IS REDUCED TO ABOUT 1/4 CUP. IT SHOULD HAVE A SYRUPY CONSISTENCY. STIR IN THE CREAM AND SET ASIDE.

MEANWHILE, HEAT REMAINING STOCK TO A BOIL. ADD NOODLES AND COOK JUST UNTIL TENDER. BLEND FLOUR WITH WATER UNTIL SMOOTH. STIR INTO NOODLES. STIR UNTIL MIXTURE BOILS 1 OR 2 MINUTES. ADD CREAM MIXTURE AND CHICKEN. SEASON WITH SALT AND PEPPER. HEAT TO SERVING TEMPERATURE. GARNISH WITH CHOPPED PARSLEY.

THE CHICKEN STOCK FOR THIS SOUP SHOULD BE RICH AND HOMEMADE SINCE THAT IS THE PRINCIPAL FLAVOR.

Spinach Vichyssoise

(MAKES 12 CUPS)

1 QUART DICED POTATOES

1 CUP DICED LEEK OR ONION

1/4 CUP BUTTER

1-1/4 CUPS WATER

1 BAG (10 OUNCES) FRESH SPINACH, WASHED AND DRAINED

3 CUPS MILK

1 CUP HEAVY CREAM

3 CUPS CHICKEN STOCK

1 TABLESPOON SALT

1/4 TEASPOON NUTMEG

1/4 TEASPOON PEPPER

SOUR CREAM

COMBINE POTATOES, LEEK, BUTTER AND WATER IN LARGE SAUCEPAN. BRING TO BOIL. COVER AND SIMMER ABOUT 30 MINUTES, OR UNTIL VEGETABLES ARE VERY TENDER. ADD SPINACH AND CONTINUE COOKING JUST UNTIL SPINACH IS WILTED. ADD MILK.

PUT SPINACH MIXTURE IN BLENDER, A LITTLE AT A TIME, AND BLEND UNTIL NOT QUITE SMOOTH. POUR INTO SOUP POT WITH CREAM AND STOCK. SEASON WITH SALT, NUTMEG, AND PEPPER. HEAT TO SERVING TEMPERATURE, OR CHILL TO SERVE COLD. SERVE GARNISHED WITH SOUR CREAM.

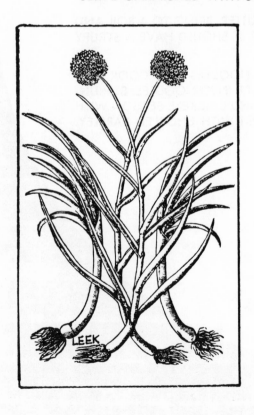
LEEK

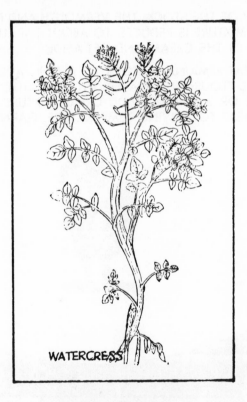
WATERCRESS

SPINACH

WATERCRESS SOUP

SUBSTITUTE 2 BUNCHES OF WATERCRESS FOR SPINACH, AND OMIT NUTMEG. PROCEED AS DIRECTED. SERVE GARNISHED WITH WATERCRESS SPRIGS IN PLACE OF SOUR CREAM.

Ukrainian Borscht

SOME BORSCHTS ARE COLD, THIN BEET SOUPS. THIS ONE IS A THICK, HOT BEEF AND VEGETABLE SOUP THAT ONLY INCIDENTALLY HAS SOME BEETS IN IT.

(MAKES ABOUT 16 CUPS)

2 TABLESPOONS VEGETABLE OIL

2 TABLESPOONS BUTTER

1 CUP CHOPPED ONION

1 TEASPOON MINCED GARLIC

3/4 POUND BEETS (WEIGHED WITHOUT TOPS), PEELED AND SHREDDED

1 CUP SHREDDED CELERY ROOT OR CHOPPED CELERY

1 CUP GRATED PARSLEY ROOT OR 2/3 CUP CHOPPED PARSLEY

1 CUP GRATED PARSNIP

2 TEASPOONS SUGAR

1/4 CUP RED WINE VINEGAR

1 CAN (1 POUND) TOMATOES, BROKEN UP

1 TABLESPOON SALT

1 QUART DICED POTATOES

2 QUARTS BEEF STOCK

1 POUND SHREDDED CABBAGE (6 QUARTS, LOOSELY PACKED)

2 CUPS DICED COOKED BEEF (BRISKET OR SHANK MEAT)

CHOPPED PARSLEY AND SOUR CREAM

HEAT OIL AND BUTTER IN HEAVY SAUCEPAN. ADD ONION AND GARLIC. SAUTE ABOUT 5 MINUTES. ADD SHREDDED OR CHOPPED VEGETABLES (NOT CABBAGE), THE SUGAR, VINEGAR, TOMATOES AND SALT. COVER AND SIMMER ABOUT 30 MINUTES.

MEANWHILE, ADD POTATOES AND STOCK TO SOUP POT. BRING TO A BOIL AND SIMMER UNTIL POTATOES ARE JUST TENDER. ADD CABBAGE, COOKED BEET MIXTURE, AND DICED BEEF. BRING TO A BOIL; REDUCE HEAT AND SIMMER 20 TO 30 MINUTES. SEASON TO TASTE WITH SALT AND PEPPER. SERVE GARNISHED WITH SOUR CREAM AND PARSLEY.

Vichyssoise

3 CUPS DICED, PEELED POTATOES
3 CUPS SLICED LEEK
2 QUARTS CHICKEN STOCK

1 CUP HEAVY CREAM
SALT AND PEPPER TO TASTE
CHOPPED FRESH CHIVES

COMBINE POTATOES, LEEK AND STOCK IN SAUCEPAN. BRING TO A BOIL AND SIMMER UNTIL VEGETABLES ARE VERY TENDER.

PUREE VEGETABLES WITH A FOOD MILL, THEN STRAIN THROUGH A SIEVE. BEAT IN CREAM AND SEASON TO TASTE WITH SALT AND PEPPER. CHILL THOROUGHLY. TASTE FOR SEASONINGS AGAIN AND THIN WITH ADDITIONAL CREAM, IF NECESSARY. SERVE WITH CHOPPED CHIVES.

WATER CAN REPLACE THE CHICKEN STOCK BUT THE STOCK GIVES A RICHER TASTE. SOME PEOPLE USE A BLENDER TO PUREE THIS SOUP, BUT WE THINK IT MAKES THE TEXTURE TOO SMOOTH.

Virginia's Broccoli Soup

(MAKES 6 CUPS)

1/2 CUP COARSELY CHOPPED ONION
1-1/4 TEASPOONS CURRY POWDER
1/4 CUP BUTTER
2 TABLESPOONS CORNSTARCH
3 CUPS MILK
1 CUP BOILING WATER

1 QUART CHOPPED FRESH BROCCOLI, OR 2 PACKAGES (10 OUNCES EACH) FROZEN BROCCOLI
1/2 TEASPOON OREGANO
SALT AND PEPPER TO TASTE
THINLY SLICED LEMON

SAUTE ONION WITH CURRY POWDER IN BUTTER UNTIL CRISP-TENDER. BLEND IN CORNSTARCH. ADD 2 CUPS OF THE MILK AND COOK, STIRRING CONSTANTLY UNTIL MIXTURE BOILS 1 TO 2 MINUTES. POUR INTO BLENDER JAR AND LET COOL A FEW MINUTES. BLEND UNTIL SMOOTH.

ADD BOILING WATER TO BROCCOLI AND COOK UNTIL JUST TENDER. PUT BROCCOLI, ONE-HALF AT A TIME, IN BLENDER JAR AND BLEND WITH REMAINING MILK UNTIL NOT QUITE SMOOTH. COMBINE BLENDED BROCCOLI AND ONION MIXTURES IN SOUP POT. ADD OREGANO AND SALT AND PEPPER TO TASTE. HEAT TO SERVING TEMPERATURE. SERVE GARNISHED WITH LEMON SLICES.

Winter Bean Soup

(MAKES 12 CUPS)

1 POUND YELLOW-EYE BEANS
WATER
1/3 CUP BUTTER
2-1/2 CUPS CHOPPED ONION
1-1/4 CUPS CHOPPED CARROT
1-1/4 CUPS CHOPPED CELERY AND LEAVES

1/4 CUP CHOPPED PARSLEY
1/2 TEASPOON MARJORAM
1/4 CUP DRY WHITE WINE
SALT AND PEPPER
CHOPPED CHIVES

SORT BEANS, THEN WASH AND SOAK IN WATER TO COVER OVERNIGHT. DRAIN. PLACE BEANS IN SOUP POT WITH 4 QUARTS WATER. BRING TO A BOIL, THEN SIMMER FOR 2 TO 3 HOURS, OR UNTIL BEANS ARE STARTING TO FALL APART.

MEANWHILE, HEAT BUTTER IN SKILLET. ADD VEGETABLES AND PARSLEY. SAUTE UNTIL CRISP-TENDER. ADD SAUTEED VEGETABLES AND MARJORAM TO SOUP. COOK 1 HOUR. LET COOL OVERNIGHT. REHEAT WITH WINE AND SEASON TO TASTE WITH SALT AND PEPPER.

SERVE GARNISHED WITH CHOPPED CHIVES.

Winter Squash Soup

(MAKES ABOUT 10 CUPS)

2 POUNDS BUTTERNUT SQUASH
1 CUP WATER
1 TEASPOON SALT
1 CUP CHOPPED ONION
1/2 SMALL CLOVE GARLIC, MINCED
2 TABLESPOONS BUTTER

2 CUPS MILK
2 CUPS LIGHT CREAM
1/2 CUP MEDIUM DRY SHERRY
SALT AND PEPPER TO TASTE
TOASTED SLICED ALMONDS

PEEL, SEED AND DICE SQUASH. COMBINE WITH WATER AND 1 TEASPOON SALT IN SAUCEPAN. BRING TO A BOIL AND SIMMER COVERED UNTIL SQUASH IS VERY TENDER.

MEANWHILE, SAUTE ONION AND GARLIC IN BUTTER UNTIL TENDER. LIQUIFY SQUASH AND ONIONS WITH MILK AND CREAM IN BLENDER. ADD SHERRY AND SALT AND PEPPER TO TASTE TO SOUP. HEAT TO SERVING TEMPERATURE. SERVE GARNISHED WITH TOASTED ALMONDS.

Zucchini Cream Soup

(MAKES ABOUT 10 CUPS)

1 CUP BOILING WATER

1 TEASPOON SALT

2 POUNDS FRESH YOUNG ZUCCHINI, DICED

2 CUPS MILK

1 CUP CHOPPED ONION

1/2 SMALL CLOVE GARLIC, MINCED

2 TABLESPOONS BUTTER

2 CUPS LIGHT CREAM

1 TEASPOON SUGAR

SALT AND PEPPER TO TASTE

SOUR CREAM

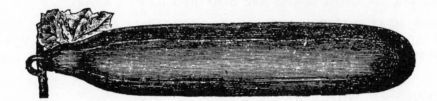

ADD WATER AND 1 TEASPOON SALT TO ZUCCHINI IN SAUCEPAN. BRING TO A BOIL; COVER AND SIMMER JUST UNTIL ZUCCHINI IS TENDER. ADD 2 CUPS OF MILK TO STOP THE COOKING.

MEANWHILE, SAUTE ONION AND GARLIC IN THE BUTTER UNTIL TENDER. BLEND COOKED ZUCCHINI AND ONION IN BLENDER JUST UNTIL SMOOTH. ADD CREAM, SUGAR, AND SALT AND PEPPER TO TASTE. HEAT TO SERVING TEMPERATURE OR CHILL AND SERVE VERY COLD. EITHER WAY, SERVE GARNISHED WITH SOUR CREAM.

Variations

SUMMER OR YELLOW SQUASH SOUP

SUBSTITUTE YELLOW OR SUMMER SQUASH FOR ZUCCHINI. SERVE GARNISHED WITH CHOPPED PARSLEY AS WELL AS SOUR CREAM.

FRESH ASPARAGUS SOUP

SUBSTITUTE FRESH ASPARAGUS FOR ZUCCHINI AND OMIT THE GARLIC. CLEAN ASPAR-AGUS, DISCARDING TOUGH ENDS. CUT OFF TIP ENDS AND PLACE IN SAUCEPAN. ADD BOILING WATER AND SALT. BOIL ABOUT 5 MINUTES OR JUST UNTIL CRISP-TENDER. RE-MOVE TIPS AND SET ASIDE. DICE REMAINING ASPARAGUS AND PREPARE AS DIRECTED FOR ZUCCHINI CREAM SOUP. ADD COOKED TIPS TO SOUP JUST BEFORE SERVING. OMIT SOUR CREAM GARNISH.

FRESH SNOWPEA SOUP

SUBSTITUTE FRESH SNOWPEAS FOR ZUCCHINI AND OMIT GARLIC. RESERVE A FEW OF THE SMALLEST SNOWPEAS FOR GARNISH, THEN PROCEED AS DIRECTED FOR ZUCCHINI CREAM SOUP. PUT BLENDED SOUP THROUGH MEDIUM MESH SIEVE BEFORE SERVING. GARNISH WITH RESERVED SNOWPEAS.

Zuppa Mariata

(MAKES 10 CUPS)

1 CUP CHOPPED FRESH MUSHROOMS (1/4 POUND)

1/2 CUP SLICED GREEN ONIONS

2 TABLESPOONS OLIVE OIL

1 TEASPOON LEMON JUICE

1/4 TEASPOON SALT

1/4 TEASPOON OREGANO

1/4 TEASPOON PEPPER

8 CUPS CHICKEN STOCK

3 OUNCES EGG PASTINA (3/4 CUP)

40 CHICKEN BALLS

2 EGG YOLKS

1 CUP LIGHT CREAM

1/4 CUP GRATED PARMESAN CHEESE

SALT, PEPPER AND OREGANO TO TASTE

SAUTE MUSHROOMS AND ONIONS IN OIL IN SKILLET UNTIL TENDER. SPRINKLE WITH LEMON JUICE, SALT, OREGANO AND PEPPER WHILE COOKING.

MEANWHILE, HEAT CHICKEN STOCK TO BOILING POINT. ADD MUSHROOM MIXTURE AND PASTINA. BOIL 2 TO 3 MINUTES. ADD CHICKEN BALLS AND CONTINUE COOKING UNTIL BALLS ARE DONE. TURN OFF HEAT AND COMBINE YOLKS, CREAM AND CHEESE. BLEND WELL AND WHISK OR BEAT INTO HOT SOUP. SEASON WITH SALT, PEPPER AND ADDITIONAL OREGANO TO TASTE. WHISK WHILE HEATING TO SERVING TEMPERATURE. SERVE GARNISHED WITH CHOPPED PARSLEY.

CHICKEN BALLS

(MAKES ABOUT 40)

1 CUP GROUND, BONED CHICKEN BREASTS

2 TABLESPOONS CHOPPED PARSLEY

2 EGG WHITES

1/2 CUP FINE DRY BREAD CRUMBS

1 TABLESPOON GRATED PARMESAN CHEESE

1/4 TEASPOON SALT

1/4 TEASPOON PEPPER

COMBINE ALL INGREDIENTS AND BLEND VERY WELL. CHILL UNTIL FIRM ENOUGH TO HANDLE. SHAPE INTO SMALL BALLS. CHILL.

COOK BALLS, EITHER IN THE SOUP OR IN BOILING SALTED WATER, UNTIL THEY FLOAT TO THE TOP, ABOUT 10 MINUTES. COOKED BALLS FREEZE VERY WELL.

Thyme.

Salads

SALADS STARTED OUT AT THE SOUP BOWL AS A KIND OF STEPCHILD
WE WERE OPEN WE FOUND NOT EVERYONE LIKED COLD SOUPS, SO
SINCE THEN OUR SALAD MENU HAS GROWN AND NOW INCLUDES SIDE SA
ALSO SERVE, IN THE SUMMER, MEAL-SIZE SALADS. HERE AGAIN, FRESH INC

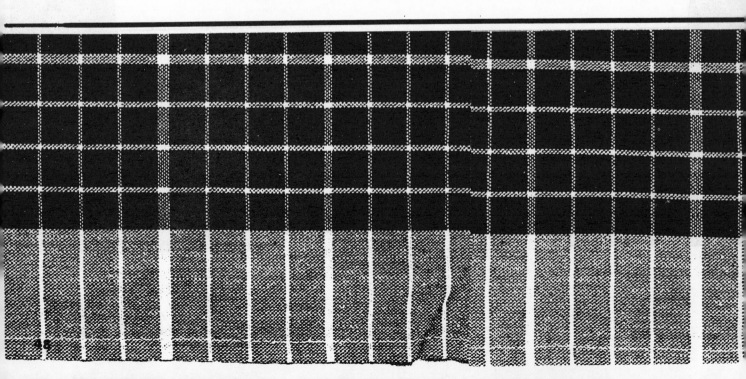

Salad Introduction

JR MENU BUT HAVE BECOME MORE AND MORE POPULAR. THE FIRST SUMMER
ARTED SERVING A COUPLE OF SALADS AS WELL AS HOT AND COLD SOUPS.
JCH AS THE FRESH MUSHROOM, GREEK, AND MARINATED BEAN SALADS. WE
NTS, FRESHLY PREPARED, ARE ESSENTIAL.

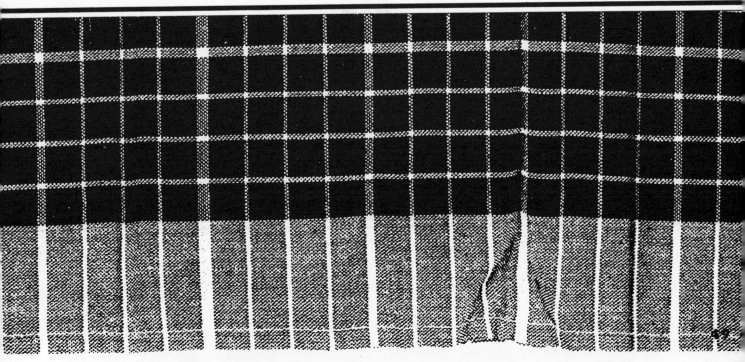

California Salad Bowl

(MAKES 10 SERVINGS)

1-1/2 QUARTS TORN ESCAROLE OR CHICORY

1 QUART TORN ICEBERG LETTUCE (1 MEDIUM HEAD)

1/2 CUP SLICED SCALLIONS

1 POUND BACON

1-1/2 MEDIUM AVOCADOS

1 TABLESPOON LEMON JUICE

1-1/2 CUPS CHOPPED COOKED CHICKEN

1/2 CUP CRUMBLED BLUE CHEESE

3/4 TO 1 CUP CURRY DRESSING TO TASTE

COMBINE ESCAROLE, LETTUCE AND SCALLIONS IN PLASTIC BAG. CHILL UNTIL READY TO SERVE.

COOK BACON UNTIL VERY CRISP. DRAIN ON PAPER TOWELS, THEN CRUMBLE COARSELY. PEEL AVOCADOS, CUT IN HALF AND REMOVE SEEDS. SPRINKLE WITH LEMON JUICE.

WHEN READY TO SERVE, PLACE GREENS IN BOWL. DICE AVOCADO. ARRANGE ROWS OF AVOCADO, BACON, CHICKEN AND BLUE CHEESE OVER GREENS. POUR CURRY DRESSING OVER ALL AND TOSS WELL.

CURRY DRESSING

COMBINE 1/4 CUP VINEGAR, 1 TABLESPOON WATER, 2/3 CUP VEGETABLE OIL, 1/2 TEASPOON SALT, 1/8 TEASPOON PEPPER, 1 TEASPOON SUGAR AND 1/4 TEASPOON CURRY POWDER IN JAR. COVER AND SHAKE WELL. SHAKE AGAIN JUST BEFORE TOSSING WITH SALAD. (MAKES ONE CUP.)

Curried Chicken and Rice Salad

(MAKES ABOUT 4 SERVINGS)

1-1/4 CUPS LONG GRAIN RICE
1 TEASPOON SALT
3 CUPS COLD WATER
1/2 TEASPOON MINCED FRESH GINGER ROOT
1 CUP DICED COOKED CHICKEN
1 CUP COOKED PEAS OR GREEN BEANS
1/2 CUP CHOPPED CELERY
1/4 CUP SLICED SCALLIONS

1/4 CUP CHOPPED PARSLEY
1/2 CUP CHOPPED GREEN PEPPER
1/2 CUP RAISINS
1-1/4 CUPS MAYONNAISE
1/4 CUP LIGHT CREAM
2 TEASPOONS CURRY POWDER
SALAD GREENS
TOASTED PEANUTS AND COCONUT

COMBINE RICE, SALT, WATER AND GINGER IN HEAVY SAUCEPAN. BRING TO A BOIL, THEN STIR WITH A FORK. COVER, REDUCE HEAT AND SIMMER ABOUT 15 MINUTES, OR UNTIL RICE IS TENDER AND WATER IS ABSORBED. COOL.

COMBINE COOLED RICE, CHICKEN, COOKED AND RAW VEGETABLES AND RAISINS. COMBINE MAYONNAISE, CREAM AND CURRY POWDER; BEAT UNTIL BLENDED. POUR OVER RICE SALAD AND MIX VERY WELL. CHILL. SERVE IN BOWLS LINED WITH SALAD GREENS. SERVE GENEROUSLY GARNISHED WITH TOASTED PEANUTS AND TOASTED COCONUT.

Greek Salad

(MAKES ABOUT 6 SERVINGS)

2 POUNDS RIPE TOMATOES

1 CUP SLICED ONION

1 CUP COARSELY DICED CUCUMBER

1/2 CUP RIPE OLIVES

3/4 CUP COARSELY DICED GREEN PEPPER

1/4 TEASPOON OREGANO

1/4 TEASPOON BASIL

1/2 POUND FETA CHEESE, DICED

1/4 CUP WINE VINEGAR

1/2 CUP OLIVE OIL

SALT AND PEPPER TO TASTE

DICE TOMATOES COARSELY. COMBINE TOMATOES, VEGETABLES, OLIVES, HERBS, CHEESE, VINEGAR AND OIL. MIX LIGHTLY. SEASON TO TASTE WITH SALT AND PEPPER. CHILL SEVERAL HOURS BEFORE SERVING.

Marinated Bean Salad

(MAKES 6 TO 8 SERVINGS)

2/3 CUP SUGAR

1 CUP VINEGAR

1/2 CUP VEGETABLE OIL

1 TEASPOON SALT

1/4 TEASPOON PEPPER

3 CANS (1 POUND EACH) CUT GREEN BEANS

1 MEDIUM RED ONION, SLICED

COMBINE SUGAR, VINEGAR, OIL, SALT AND PEPPER; BEAT OR SHAKE WELL. COMBINE BEANS AND ONION IN BOWL; POUR DRESSING OVER BEANS AND TOSS LIGHTLY. CHILL AT LEAST 24 HOURS, STIRRING OCCASIONALLY.

Lebanese Salad

THE ONLY THING ABOUT THIS SALAD THAT'S LEBANESE IS THE NAME — BUT IT IS A VERY GOOD SALAD.

(MAKES 8 SERVINGS)

2 CUPS BROWN LENTILS

1/2 CUP CHOPPED DILL PICKLES

1/4 CUP SLICED SCALLIONS

8 FLAT ANCHOVY FILLETS, CHOPPED

3 TABLESPOONS CHOPPED CAPERS

2 TABLESPOONS MINCED PARSLEY

5 TABLESPOONS WINE VINEGAR

12 TABLESPOONS OLIVE OIL

1/2 TEASPOON TARRAGON LEAVES

6 CUPS DICED ZUCCHINI

2 MEDIUM AVOCADOS

1/2 CUP MINCED ONION

1 CUP MINCED CELERY

1 CLOVE GARLIC, MINCED

SALT AND PEPPER

SALAD GREENS

3 TOMATOES, CUT IN EIGHTHS

4 HARD-COOKED EGGS, HALVED

COVER LENTILS WITH WATER AND SOAK 1 TO 2 HOURS. DRAIN. ADD FRESH SALTED WATER. BRING TO A BOIL AND COOK JUST UNTIL TENDER. DRAIN. ADD PICKLES, SCALLIONS, ANCHOVIES, CAPERS, PARSLEY, 4 TABLESPOONS VINEGAR, 8 TABLESPOONS OLIVE OIL AND THE TARRAGON. MIX VERY WELL AND CHILL.

COOK DICED ZUCCHINI IN A LITTLE SALTED WATER <u>JUST</u> UNTIL TENDER. DRAIN AND SPREAD OUT ON A TRAY TO COOL QUICKLY.

PEEL, SEED AND DICE AVOCADO. COMBINE ZUCCHINI, AVOCADO, ONION, CELERY, GARLIC, REMAINING 1 TABLESPOON VINEGAR AND 1/4 CUP OLIVE OIL. MIX WELL AND SEASON TO TASTE WITH SALT AND PEPPER. CHILL.

WHEN READY TO SERVE, MOUND LENTIL AND ZUCCHINI MIXTURES IN BOWLS LINED WITH SALAD GREENS. SERVE GARNISHED WITH TOMATOES, HARD-COOKED EGGS AND CHOPPED PARSLEY, IF DESIRED.

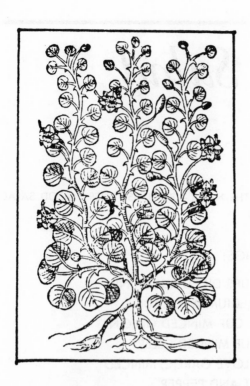

Mary's Summer Salad

(MAKES ABOUT 6 SERVINGS)

4 CUPS COOKED GARBANZO BEANS*
1 CUP CHOPPED CELERY
1/2 CUP FINELY CHOPPED ONION
2 HARD-COOKED EGGS, CHOPPED
1/2 CUP CHOPPED PIMIENTO
1 CAN (7 OUNCES) TUNA, DRAINED

1 TABLESPOON CHOPPED CAPERS
1/2 CUP BASIL DRESSING (P. 71)
1 CUP MAYONNAISE
SALT AND PEPPER
SALAD GREENS
CHOPPED PARSLEY

COMBINE GARBANZO BEANS, CELERY, ONION, EGGS, PIMIENTO, TUNA, CAPERS, BASIL DRESSING AND MAYONNAISE. MIX VERY WELL. SEASON TO TASTE WITH SALT AND PEPPER. SERVE IN BOWLS LINED WITH SALAD GREENS AND GARNISH WITH CHOPPED PARSLEY.

* USE EITHER DRIED OR CANNED GARBANZOS. IF USING DRIED, SOAK 1-1/2 CUPS BEANS OVERNIGHT IN WATER TO COVER. DRAIN, THEN SIMMER UNTIL TENDER IN SALTED WATER. DRAIN AND CHILL.

Mediterranean Salad

THIS SALAD IS MADE UP OF RATATOUILLE AND MARINATED BEANS. THE RECIPE LOOKS LONG, BUT IT'S NOT DIFFICULT, AND IT IS A DELICIOUS SALAD.

(MAKES 6 SERVINGS)

1 MEDIUM EGGPLANT, CUT IN STRIPS
3/4 POUND ZUCCHINI, CUT IN STRIPS
1 TABLESPOON SALT
1 CUP SLICED ONION
1 CUP DICED GREEN PEPPER
1 LARGE CLOVE GARLIC, MINCED
1/4 CUP OLIVE OIL
1 POUND TOMATOES, PEELED AND SEEDED
DASH GROUND CORIANDER

SALT AND PEPPER TO TASTE
1-3/4 CUPS DRY YELLOW-EYE BEANS OR MARROW BEANS
3/4 CUP BASIL DRESSING (P. 71)
5 TABLESPOONS CHOPPED PARSLEY
2 TABLESPOONS CHOPPED FRESH BASIL
SALAD GREENS
6 HARD-COOKED EGGS, HALVED
1 CUCUMBER, SCORED AND SLICED

COMBINE EGGPLANT, ZUCCHINI AND SALT IN BOWL. WEIGHT DOWN WITH ANOTHER BOWL FILLED WITH SOMETHING HEAVY AND LET STAND 1 HOUR. DRAIN, THEN DRY VEGETABLES ON PAPER TOWELS.

MEANWHILE, SAUTE ONION, GREEN PEPPER AND GARLIC IN OLIVE OIL IN HEAVY SAUCEPAN UNTIL WILTED. ADD EGGPLANT-ZUCCHINI MIXTURE AND SIMMER, STIRRING FREQUENTLY, ABOUT 30 MINUTES. CUT TOMATOES IN STRIPS AND ADD TO SIMMERING MIXTURE. CONTINUE TO COOK UNTIL EGGPLANT IS JUST TENDER, 20 TO 30 MINUTES. STIR FREQUENTLY. ADD CORIANDER AND SALT AND PEPPER TO TASTE. COOL, THEN CHILL.

NEXT ADD SALTED WATER TO BEANS TO COVER. BRING TO A BOIL AND BOIL 2 MINUTES. TURN OFF HEAT. COVER AND LET STAND 1 HOUR. BRING TO A BOIL AGAIN AND SIMMER BEANS UNTIL TENDER, ADDING MORE WATER, IF NECESSARY. DRAIN. ADD BASIL DRESSING AND A TABLESPOON EACH OF THE PARSLEY AND BASIL. MIX WELL AND CHILL.

STIR REMAINING 1/4 CUP PARSLEY AND 1 TABLESPOON BASIL INTO THE CHILLED EGGPLANT MIXTURE. MOUND CHILLED EGGPLANT AND BEAN MIXTURES IN BOWLS LINED WITH SALAD GREENS AND GARNISH WITH EGGS AND CUCUMBER.

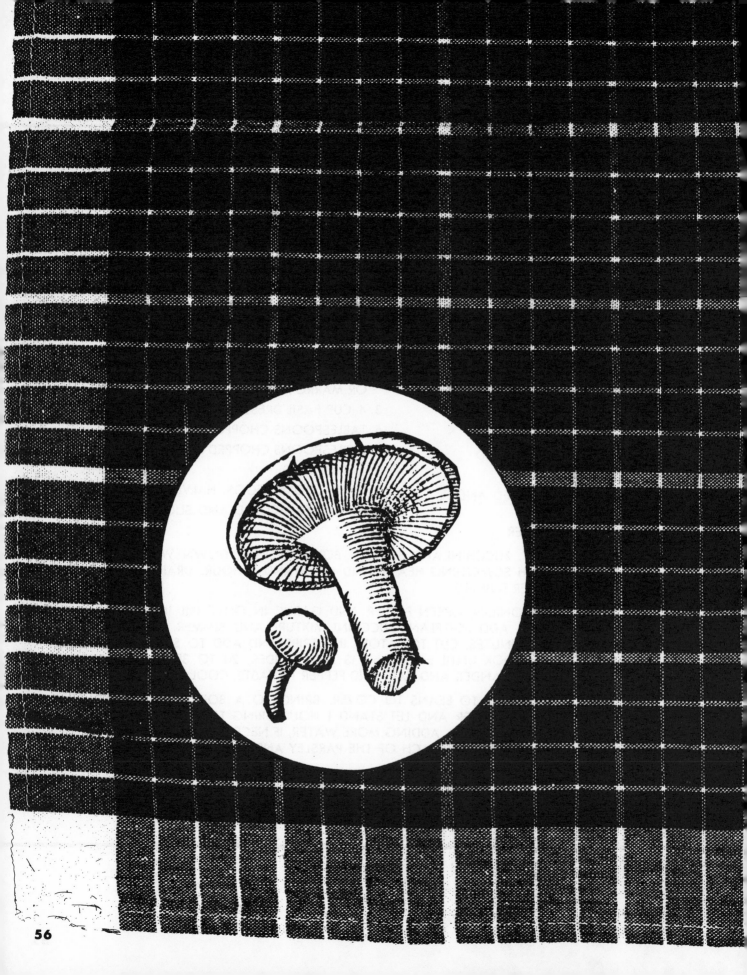

Fresh Mushroom Salad

(MAKES 6 SERVINGS)

2 TABLESPOONS LEMON JUICE

1 TEASPOON SALT

1/4 TEASPOON PEPPER

1 CLOVE GARLIC, SCORED

10 TABLESPOONS OLIVE OIL

6 CUPS SLICED FRESH MUSHROOMS

SALAD GREENS

CHOPPED PARSLEY

COMBINE LEMON JUICE, SALT, PEPPER, GARLIC AND OLIVE OIL. BEAT OR SHAKE WELL. LET STAND 30 MINUTES TO 1 HOUR. REMOVE GARLIC. TOSS DRESSING WITH MUSHROOMS. ARRANGE SALAD GREENS ON SERVING PLATES AND TOP WITH MUSHROOMS. SPRINKLE WITH CHOPPED PARSLEY.

Oriental Salad

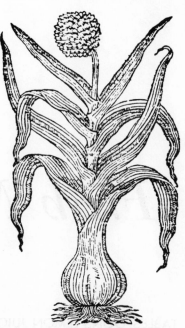

FRESH BEAN SPROUTS — MUNG BEANS — ARE ABOUT 500% BETTER THAN THE CANNED VARIETY. THE NEW YORK TIMES NATURAL FOODS COOKBOOK, BY JEAN HEWITT, HAS GOOD DIRECTIONS FOR SPROUTING BEANS AND GRAINS.

2 POUNDS CHICKEN BREASTS, SKINNED AND BONED

1/4 CUP SOY SAUCE

2/3 CUP SALAD OIL

1 CLOVE GARLIC, SCORED

1 TEASPOON GRATED LEMON PEEL

1/4 CUP LEMON JUICE

1 PACKAGE (10 OUNCES) FRESH SPINACH

7 CUPS SHREDDED ICEBERG LETTUCE (1 LARGE HEAD)

3 CUPS FRESH BEAN SPROUTS

1/2 TEASPOON SALT

1/4 CUP TOASTED SESAME SEED

(MAKES 6-8 SERVINGS)

CUT CHICKEN INTO 2-INCH STRIPS. ADD 1 TABLESPOON OF THE SOY SAUCE, 2 TABLESPOONS OIL, THE GARLIC AND HALF THE LEMON PEEL TO THE CHICKEN IN A BOWL. MIX WELL AND CHILL SEVERAL HOURS.

HEAT ANOTHER 2 TABLESPOONS OF THE OIL IN A SKILLET. ADD CHICKEN STRIPS A FEW AT A TIME AND SAUTE 3 TO 5 MINUTES, OR UNTIL STRIPS BECOME FIRM. DON'T OVERCOOK. DISCARD GARLIC CLOVE.

COMBINE COOKED CHICKEN AND ALL REMAINING OIL, SOY SAUCE AND LEMON PEEL. ADD LEMON JUICE AND MIX WELL. CHILL.

PICK OFF STEMS FROM SPINACH; WASH AND DRAIN THOROUGHLY. CHOP SPINACH AND COMBINE WITH LETTUCE AND BEAN SPROUTS. CHILL. WHEN READY TO SERVE, SPRINKLE GREENS WITH SALT AND SESAME SEED. TOSS WITH CHICKEN MIXTURE AND SERVE IMMEDIATELY.

Pennsylvania Dutch Salad

(MAKES 8 SERVINGS)

1 BAG (10 OUNCES) FRESH SPINACH

1-1/4 POUNDS SLICED BACON

1-1/2 HEADS ICEBERG LETTUCE, SHREDDED

1-1/2 CUPS SLICED SCALLIONS

8 HARD-COOKED EGGS, CHOPPED

2/3 TO 3/4 CUP SWEET AND SOUR DRESSING (P. 71)

PICK OFF STEMS FROM SPINACH AND DISCARD. WASH LEAVES, THEN DRAIN WELL. CHOP COARSELY AND CHILL.

COOK BACON UNTIL CRISP. DRAIN ON PAPER TOWELS AND CRUMBLE. WHEN READY TO SERVE, COMBINE SPINACH, LETTUCE AND SCALLIONS IN SALAD BOWL. SPRINKLE WITH EGGS AND BACON. TOSS WITH DRESSING AND SERVE AT ONCE.

Salade Niçoise

SMALL, NEW POTATOES, COOKED JUST UNTIL TENDER, MAKE THE BEST TASTING SALAD.

(MAKES 6 SERVINGS)

1 QUART SLICED COOKED POTATOES

1 PACKAGE (10 OUNCES) FROZEN CUT GREEN BEANS, COOKED

1-1/2 TO 2 CUPS BASIL DRESSING (P. 71)

SALAD GREENS

3 MEDIUM TOMATOES, QUARTERED

1 CAN (7 OUNCES) TUNA, DRAINED AND BROKEN INTO CHUNKS

12 ANCHOVY FILLETS

3 HARD-COOKED EGGS, HALVED

6 GREEN PEPPER RINGS

24 RIPE OLIVES

COMBINE POTATOES, GREEN BEANS AND 1/2 CUP OF THE BASIL DRESSING. MIX WELL AND CHILL SEVERAL HOURS OR OVERNIGHT.

LINE SERVING BOWLS WITH SALAD GREENS. MOUND POTATO SALAD IN THE CENTER OF EACH. ARRANGE REMAINING INGREDIENTS IN BOWL AROUND POTATO SALAD. SERVE WITH REMAINING BASIL DRESSING.

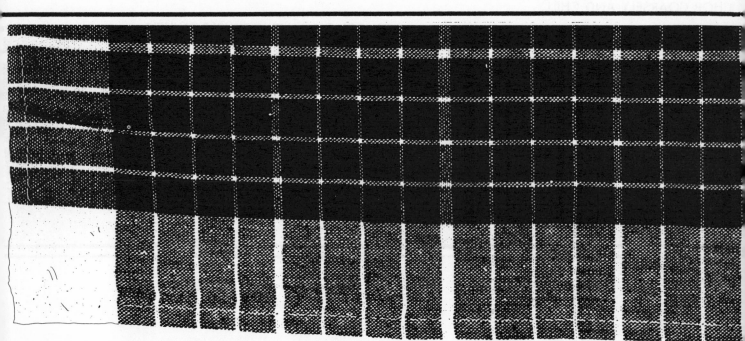

Spanish Salad

(MAKES 6 SERVINGS)

1 CUP DICED COOKED POTATOES

1-1/2 CUPS DICED COOKED CARROTS

1-1/2 CUPS COOKED CUT GREEN BEANS

1-1/2 CUPS COOKED PEAS

1 CUP DICED COOKED BEETS

1 CUP THINLY SLICED CELERY

1/4 CUP CHOPPED ONION

2 HARD-COOKED EGGS, CHOPPED

3/4 CUP CHOPPED STUFFED GREEN OLIVES

3/4 CUP MAYONNAISE

1/4 CUP CHILI SAUCE

1 TEASPOON LEMON JUICE

SALT AND PEPPER TO TASTE

SALAD GREENS

COMBINE COOKED AND RAW VEGETABLES, EGGS AND OLIVES. COMBINE MAYONNAISE, CHILI SAUCE AND LEMON JUICE. MIX WELL AND TOSS WITH VEGETABLES. SEASON TO TASTE WITH SALT AND PEPPER. CHILL. WHEN READY TO SERVE, MOUND SALAD IN BOWLS LINED WITH SALAD GREENS. SPRINKLE WITH CHOPPED PARSLEY, IF DESIRED.

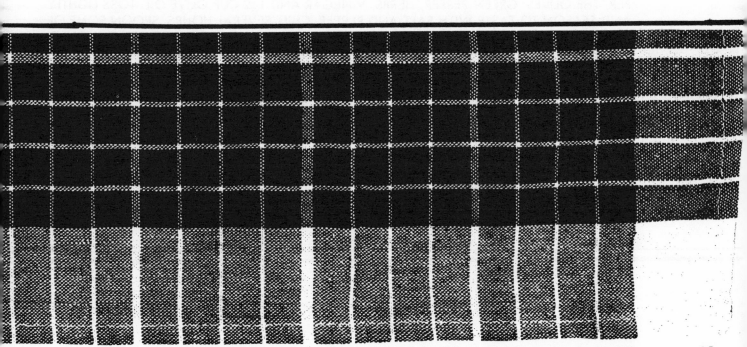

Tabooli Salad

(MAKES 6 TO 8 SERVINGS)

1 CUP BULGAR

3/4 CUP BOILING WATER

2/3 CUP MINCED ONION

1/4 CUP CHOPPED PARSLEY

1 CUP FINELY CHOPPED CUCUMBER

1 CUP MINCED CELERY

1-1/2 TABLESPOONS CHOPPED MINT

6 TABLESPOONS OLIVE OIL

2 TABLESPOONS LEMON JUICE

SALT AND PEPPER

2 POUNDS RIPE TOMATOES

1 CUP SLICED ONION

1 CUP DICED CUCUMBER

1/2 CUP RIPE OLIVES

3/4 CUP DICED GREEN PEPPER

1/4 TEASPOON EACH: BASIL AND OREGANO

1/4 CUP WINE VINEGAR

1/2 CUP OLIVE OIL

SALAD GREENS

3/4 TO 1 POUND FETA CHEESE, DICED

COMBINE BULGAR AND BOILING WATER; LET STAND TO LUKEWARM. ADD MINCED ONION, PARSLEY, FINELY CHOPPED CUCUMBER, CELERY, MINT, 6 TABLESPOONS OIL, THE LEMON JUICE, 1-1/2 TEASPOONS SALT AND A DASH OF PEPPER. CHILL SEVERAL HOURS OR OVERNIGHT.

DICE TOMATOES COARSELY. COMBINE TOMATOES, SLICED ONION, DICED CUCUMBER, THE OLIVES, GREEN PEPPER, HERBS, VINEGAR AND 1/2 CUP OLIVE OIL. TOSS LIGHTLY AND SEASON TO TASTE WITH SALT AND PEPPER. CHILL SEVERAL HOURS. SPOON SOME OF THE DRESSING FROM THE TOMATOES OVER THE CHEESE. WHEN READY TO SERVE, MOUND THE BULGAR AND TOMATO MIXTURES IN BOWLS LINED WITH SALAD GREENS. GARNISH WITH DICED CHEESE.

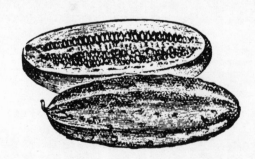

Texas Corn Salad

(MAKES 4 SERVINGS)

4 HARD-COOKED EGGS
4 CUPS WHOLE KERNEL CORN (USE CANNED OR FROZEN CORN)
1 AVOCADO, PEELED, SEEDED AND DICED
1/4 CUP SLICED SCALLIONS
1/2 CUP MAYONNAISE
1 TABLESPOON LEMON JUICE

1/2 TEASPOON CHILI POWDER
1/2 TEASPOON CUMIN
DASH NUTMEG
SALT AND PEPPER TO TASTE
SALAD GREENS
CHOPPED PARSLEY

CHOP TWO OF THE EGGS AND HALVE OR QUARTER THE OTHER TWO. COMBINE THE CHOPPED EGGS, THE CORN, AVOCADO AND SCALLIONS. BLEND MAYONNAISE, LEMON JUICE AND SPICES. POUR OVER CORN AND MIX WELL. SEASON TO TASTE WITH SALT AND PEPPER. CHILL. SPOON INTO BOWLS LINED WITH SALAD GREENS. GARNISH WITH HARD-COOKED EGGS AND CHOPPED PARSLEY.

The Salad

FOR DRAMA, ARRANGE THIS SALAD IN LAYERS IN A GLASS OR CLEAR PLASTIC SALAD BOWL. TOSS THE SALAD TOGETHER JUST BEFORE SERVING.

(MAKES 6 SERVINGS)

1 POUND SLICED BACON

7 CUPS SHREDDED ICEBERG LETTUCE (1 LARGE HEAD)

2 CUPS COOKED, DICED CARROTS

2 CUPS COOKED PEAS

3/4 CUP CHOPPED ONION

1 CUP SLICED OR CHOPPED STUFFED GREEN OLIVES

1-1/2 CUPS CHOPPED CELERY

1-1/4 CUPS HOMEMADE MAYONNAISE

COOK BACON UNTIL CRISP. DRAIN THOROUGHLY ON PAPER TOWELS; CRUMBLE COARSELY. ARRANGE LETTUCE IN THE BOTTOM OF SALAD BOWL. ARRANGE LAYERS OF VEGETABLES AND OLIVES OVER LETTUCE. TOP WITH BACON. SPREAD MAYONNAISE OVER BACON AND GARNISH WITH A FEW SLICES OF STUFFED OLIVES, IF DESIRED. CHILL UNTIL READY TO SERVE. TOSS WELL BEFORE SERVING.

Homemade Mayonnaise

(MAKES ABOUT 1 QUART)

4 EGG YOLKS

2 WHOLE EGGS

1 TEASPOON DRY MUSTARD

1-1/2 TEASPOONS SALT

1/4 CUP LEMON JUICE*

1 QUART VEGETABLE OIL**

IN SMALL BOWL OF ELECTRIC MIXER, BEAT EGG YOLKS AND WHOLE EGGS UNTIL THICK. BEAT IN MUSTARD AND SALT; THEN BEAT IN LEMON JUICE. CONTINUE BEATING FOR ABOUT 30 SECONDS, THEN START ADDING OIL, A FEW DROPS AT A TIME. CONTINUE TO ADD THE OIL IN A THIN STREAM, BEATING CONSTANTLY. AFTER ABOUT HALF THE OIL HAS BEEN ADDED, THE REST MAY BE POURED IN A LITTLE MORE RAPIDLY, BUT CONTINUE TO BEAT CONSTANTLY. CHILL.

* A MIXTURE OF PART LEMON JUICE AND VINEGAR MAY BE USED.

** OIL AT ROOM TEMPERATURE WORKS BEST. USE PART OR ALL OLIVE OIL, IF DESIRED.

Sweet and Sour Dressing

(MAKES ABOUT 2 CUPS)

2/3 CUP SUGAR
1 CUP VINEGAR
1/2 CUP VEGETABLE OIL

1 TEASPOON SALT
1/8 TEASPOON PEPPER

COMBINE ALL INGREDIENTS AND BEAT OR SHAKE WELL.

Basil Dressing

THIS IS A VERSATILE DRESSING AND IS USED IN SEVERAL SOUP BOWL SALADS. IT'S QUITE GOOD ON A PLAIN TOSSED SALAD OR ON SLICED TOMATOES.

(MAKES ABOUT 1-1/2 CUPS)

1/3 CUP WINE VINEGAR
1 TABLESPOON DRIED BASIL
3 TABLESPOONS CHOPPED PARSLEY

1-1/4 TEASPOONS SALT
1/8 TEASPOON PEPPER
1 CUP OLIVE OIL

COMBINE VINEGAR, HERBS, SALT AND PEPPER. STIR TO COMBINE. ADD OIL AND BEAT OR SHAKE UNTIL WELL BLENDED.

Breads

Bread Introduction

THE FOLLOWING BREAD RECIPES MAY BE A LITTLE TOO BRIEF FOR A BEGINNING BREAD MAKER. BUT THERE ARE MANY EXCELLENT BOOKS DETAILING BREAD-MAKING TECHNIQUES. <u>BEARD ON BREAD</u> IS GOOD AND SO ARE JULIA CHILD'S BOOKS CONTAINING BREAD RECIPES.

NOW, REGARDING SOME OF THE INGREDIENTS. WHEN A RECIPE CALLS FOR MILK, USE RECONSTITUTED DRY MILK. THIS AVOIDS THE MESSY STEP OF SCALDING. ALL OF THE RECIPES SPECIFY 8 x 4-INCH LOAF PANS, BUT USE 9 x 5-INCH PANS IF THAT'S WHAT YOU HAVE. AFTER ALL, BREAD BAKING IS VERY FLEXIBLE. MAKE THE TEMPERATURE OF THE INGREDIENTS WORK FOR YOU. ADD MARGARINE TO HOT LIQUIDS SO IT WILL MELT. IF YOU WANT TO COOL A HOT MIXTURE, USE ICE AS PART OF THE WATER.

ADD A LITTLE SUGAR, HONEY OR MOLASSES TO THE WATER IN WHICH THE YEAST IS DISSOLVED. USE THE SAME CUP MEASURE FOR DISSOLVING THE YEAST THAT WAS USED FOR THE MOLASSES OR HONEY. IF SUGAR IS USED IN THE BREAD, RESERVE A TEASPOON OF IT FOR DISSOLVING THE YEAST.

OUR BREAD DOUGHS ARE APT TO BE SOFT. IF YOU FIND THEM DIFFICULT TO KNEAD, SIMPLY ADD MORE FLOUR. OR, IF YOU PREFER, YOU CAN CHILL THE DOUGH. WHEN WE MAKE BREAD FOR THE RESTAURANT THE DOUGH USUALLY RISES TWICE — THE SECOND TIME OVERNIGHT IN THE REFRIGERATOR. THUS, WHEN THE DOUGH IS SHAPED IN THE MORNING IT IS COLDER AND FIRMER AND, CONSEQUENTLY, EASIER TO HANDLE.

THE FRENCH BREAD RECIPE WE USE IS NOT AMONG THE FOLLOWING RECIPES BECAUSE IT WOULD TAKE TOO MUCH SPACE. JULIA CHILD AND SIMONE BECK DO A DEFINITIVE JOB ON FRENCH BREAD IN THEIR <u>MASTERING THE ART OF FRENCH COOKING</u>, VOL. II. THEIRS IS THE RECIPE AND TECHNIQUE WE USE.

Barbara Wesley's Anadama Bread

(MAKES 2 LOAVES)

1/2 CUP STONE-GROUND YELLOW CORNMEAL

1 CUP COLD WATER

1 CUP BOILING WATER

3 TABLESPOONS BUTTER OR MARGARINE

1/2 CUP MOLASSES

1 PACKAGE ACTIVE DRY YEAST

1/2 CUP WARM WATER

2 TEASPOONS SALT

3 CUPS STONE-GROUND WHOLE WHEAT FLOUR

2-1/2 TO 3 CUPS UNBLEACHED WHITE FLOUR

COMBINE CORNMEAL AND 1/2 CUP COLD WATER IN SAUCEPAN; MIX WELL. ADD 1 CUP BOILING WATER WHILE STIRRING CORNMEAL. COOK AND STIR OVER MEDIUM HEAT UNTIL MIXTURE BOILS. ADD BUTTER, MOLASSES AND REMAINING 1/2 CUP COLD WATER. COOL TO LUKEWARM.

COMBINE YEAST AND WARM WATER. STIR TO BLEND AND LET STAND 5 MINUTES. ADD TO COOLED CORNMEAL MIXTURE IN MIXING BOWL. STIR IN SALT, WHOLE WHEAT FLOUR AND ENOUGH WHITE FLOUR TO PRODUCE A NON-STICKY DOUGH. TURN OUT ON FLOURED SURFACE AND KNEAD UNTIL DOUGH BECOMES SMOOTH AND ELASTIC.

PLACE DOUGH IN GREASED BOWL. TURN TO GREASE TOP. COVER AND LET RISE UNTIL DOUBLED IN BULK. PUNCH DOWN AND LET RISE AGAIN, IF DESIRED. TURN OUT ON FLOURED SURFACE AND SHAPE INTO LOAVES. PLACE IN TWO-GREASED 8 x 4-INCH LOAF PANS. COVER AND LET RISE UNTIL BREAD RISES TO TOPS OF PANS. BAKE IN PRE-HEATED 375° OVEN FOR 45 TO 55 MINUTES, OR UNTIL LOAVES ARE WELL BROWNED AND SOUND HOLLOW WHEN TAPPED ON THE BOTTOMS. REMOVE FROM PANS AND COOL ON RACKS.

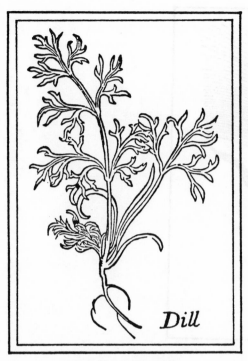

Dill

(MAKES 2 LOAVES)

2 CUPS CREAMED COTTAGE CHEESE
2 TABLESPOONS BUTTER OR MARGARINE
1 TABLESPOON DILL SEED
2 TABLESPOONS MINCED GREEN ONION
1/4 CUP SUGAR
1/4 TEASPOON BAKING SODA

2 TEASPOONS SALT
2 EGGS, BEATEN
1/2 CUP WARM WATER
1 PACKAGE ACTIVE DRY YEAST
5 CUPS UNBLEACHED FLOUR

WARM COTTAGE CHEESE AND BUTTER SLIGHTLY. ADD DILL SEED, ONION, SUGAR, BAKING SODA, SALT AND EGGS. BEAT UNTIL BLENDED.

COMBINE WATER AND YEAST; STIR AND LET STAND UNTIL DISSOLVED. STIR INTO COTTAGE CHEESE MIXTURE. STIR IN AS MUCH FLOUR AS POSSIBLE, THEN KNEAD IN THE REST. CONTINUE KNEADING UNTIL DOUGH BECOMES SMOOTH.

PLACE DOUGH IN GREASED BOWL. TURN TO GREASE TOP. COVER AND LET STAND UNTIL DOUBLED IN BULK. PUNCH DOWN. SHAPE INTO 2 LOAVES AND PLACE IN GREASED 8 x 4-INCH LOAF PANS. COVER AND LET RISE UNTIL DOUGH REACHES TOPS OF PANS. BAKE IN PRE-HEATED 375° OVEN FOR 35 TO 45 MINUTES, OR UNTIL BROWNED AND LOAVES SOUND HOLLOW WHEN TAPPED ON BOTTOM. REMOVE FROM PANS AND COOL ON RACKS.

Beverly's Dill Bread

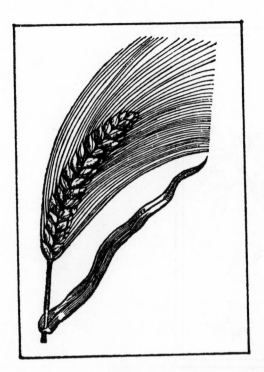

Bran Wheat Bread

(MAKES 2 LOAVES)

1 CUP BOILING WATER	3/4 CUP MILK, SCALDED
6 TABLESPOONS BUTTER OR MARGARINE	2 PACKAGES ACTIVE DRY YEAST
1 CUP ALL-BRAN CEREAL	1/2 CUP WARM WATER
3 TABLESPOONS SUGAR	2-1/2 CUPS UNBLEACHED FLOUR
1 TABLESPOON SALT	3 CUPS STONE-GROUND WHOLE WHEAT FLOUR
1/3 CUP MOLASSES	

ADD BOILING WATER TO BUTTER AND CEREAL IN MIXING BOWL. STIR TO MELT BUTTER. ADD SUGAR, SALT, MOLASSES AND MILK. COOL IF NECESSARY TO LUKEWARM.

ADD YEAST TO WARM WATER. STIR AND LET STAND TO DISSOLVE. ADD TO BRAN MIXTURE. STIR IN AS MUCH FLOUR AS POSSIBLE, THEN KNEAD IN THE REST. CONTINUE KNEADING UNTIL DOUGH IS SMOOTH. PLACE IN GREASED BOWL AND TURN TO COAT TOP. COVER AND LET RISE UNTIL DOUBLED IN BULK. PUNCH DOWN AND SHAPE INTO 2 LOAVES. PLACE IN GREASED 8 x 4-INCH PANS. LET RISE UNTIL DOUGH RISES TO TOPS OF THE PANS. BAKE IN PRE-HEATED 375° OVEN FOR ABOUT 45 MINUTES, OR UNTIL BROWNED AND LOAVES SOUND HOLLOW WHEN TAPPED ON THE BOTTOM. REMOVE FROM PANS AND COOL ON RACKS.

Cecily's Cheese Bread

(MAKES 2 LOAVES)

1-1/4 CUPS MILK, SCALDED

2 TABLESPOONS SUGAR

6 OUNCES VERMONT CHEDDAR CHEESE, GRATED (ABOUT 1-1/4 CUPS)

2 TEASPOONS SALT

1 PACKAGE ACTIVE DRY YEAST

1/2 CUP WARM WATER

4 CUPS UNBLEACHED FLOUR

COMBINE MILK AND SUGAR. COOL UNTIL LUKEWARM. ADD CHEESE AND SALT. STIR YEAST INTO WATER. LET STAND UNTIL DISSOLVED. ADD TO CHEESE MIXTURE. STIR IN AS MUCH FLOUR AS POSSIBLE, THEN KNEAD IN THE REST. CONTINUE TO KNEAD UNTIL DOUGH IS SMOOTH. PLACE IN GREASED BOWL AND TURN TO COAT TOP. COVER AND LET RISE UNTIL DOUBLED IN BULK. PUNCH DOUGH DOWN AND SHAPE INTO 2 LOAVES. PLACE IN GREASED 8 x 4-INCH PANS. COVER AND LET RISE TO TOPS OF PANS. BAKE IN PRE-HEATED 375° OVEN 35 TO 40 MINUTES, OR UNTIL BROWNED AND LOAVES SOUND HOLLOW WHEN TAPPED ON THE BOTTOMS. REMOVE FROM PANS AND COOL ON RACKS.

Cheese Bran Muffins

(MAKES ABOUT 12 MUFFINS)

1 CUP ALL-BRAN CEREAL

1-1/4 CUPS BUTTERMILK

1/4 CUP SHORTENING

1/3 CUP SUGAR

1 EGG

1-1/2 CUPS UNBLEACHED FLOUR

1-1/2 TEASPOONS BAKING POWDER

1/4 TEASPOON BAKING SODA

1/2 TEASPOON SALT

1 CUP SHREDDED CHEDDAR CHEESE

COMBINE CEREAL AND BUTTERMILK; SET ASIDE. CREAM SHORTENING AND SUGAR TOGETHER IN MIXING BOWL. BEAT IN EGG. STIR FLOUR, BAKING POWDER, SODA AND SALT TOGETHER. ADD TO CREAMED MIXTURE ALTERNATELY WITH BRAN MIXTURE. ADD CHEESE AND STIR ONLY TO MIX EVENLY. FILL GREASED MUFFIN PANS 3/4 FULL. BAKE IN PRE-HEATED 400° OVEN FOR 25 TO 30 MINUTES, OR UNTIL BROWNED.

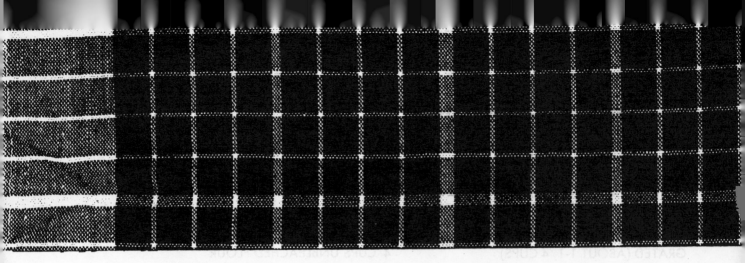

Dark Wheat Bread

(MAKES 2 LOAVES)

2-2/3 CUPS STRONG COFFEE

2/3 CUP WATER

1/3 CUP HONEY

1 TABLESPOON SALT

1 PACKAGE ACTIVE DRY YEAST

1/2 CUP WARM WATER

1/2 CUP YELLOW CORNMEAL

4-1/2 CUPS STONE-GROUND WHOLE WHEAT FLOUR

4 CUPS UNBLEACHED FLOUR

COMBINE COFFEE, 2/3 CUP WATER, THE HONEY AND SALT IN MIXING BOWL. COOL TO LUKEWARM, IF NECESSARY. STIR YEAST INTO 1/2 CUP WATER; LET STAND UNTIL DISSOLVED. ADD TO COFFEE MIXTURE. STIR IN CORNMEAL AND AS MUCH OF THE FLOUR AS POSSIBLE. KNEAD IN THE REST. CONTINUE TO KNEAD UNTIL DOUGH IS SMOOTH. PLACE IN GREASED BOWL AND TURN TO GREASE TOP. COVER AND LET RISE UNTIL DOUBLED IN BULK. PUNCH DOWN AND SHAPE INTO 2 LOAVES. PLACE IN GREASED 8 x 4-INCH PANS. COVER AND LET RISE UNTIL JUST BELOW TOPS OF PANS. BAKE IN PRE-HEATED 375° OVEN FOR 45 MINUTES, OR UNTIL BROWNED AND BREAD SOUNDS HOLLOW WHEN TAPPED ON THE BOTTOM. REMOVE FROM PANS AND COOL ON RACKS.

Granola Bread

AS FAR AS WE KNOW, GRANOLA FLOUR IS SOLD ONLY IN 50-POUND BAGS. IT'S MADE BY THE PEAVEY FLOUR MILLS IN MINNEAPOLIS, MINNESOTA 55402. AT THIS TIME THERE ARE ONE OR TWO FOOD STORES IN THIS AREA WHICH REPACK IT IN SMALLER QUANTITIES TO BE SOLD AT RETAIL.

(MAKES 3 LOAVES)

1 CUP REGULAR OATS	1/2 TEASPOON SALT
3 TABLESPOONS BUTTER OR MARGARINE	3/4 CUP WARM WATER
1 CUP BOILING WATER	1 PACKAGE ACTIVE DRY YEAST
1 CUP COLD WATER	10 CUPS GRANOLA FLOUR
1/4 CUP HONEY	3/4 CUP BROKEN WALNUTS

COMBINE OATS, BUTTER AND BOILING WATER IN MIXING BOWL. STIR TO MELT BUTTER. ADD COLD WATER, HONEY AND SALT. COMBINE WARM WATER AND YEAST; STIR TO DISSOLVE YEAST AND LET STAND FOR 5 MINUTES. STIR INTO OAT MIXTURE. STIR IN AS MUCH OF THE FLOUR AS YOU CAN, THEN ADD THE NUTS. KNEAD IN THE REMAINING FLOUR. CONTINUE KNEADING UNTIL DOUGH IS SMOOTH.

PLACE DOUGH IN GREASED BOWL AND TURN TO GREASE THE TOP. COVER AND LET RISE UNTIL DOUBLED IN BULK. PUNCH DOWN AND SHAPE INTO 3 LOAVES. PLACE IN GREASED 8 x 4-INCH LOAF PANS. COVER AND LET RISE UNTIL DOUGH COMES TO TOPS OF THE PANS. BAKE IN PRE-HEATED 375° OVEN 45 MINUTES, OR UNTIL BROWNED AND LOAVES SOUND HOLLOW WHEN TAPPED ON THE BOTTOM. REMOVE FROM PANS AND COOL ON RACKS.

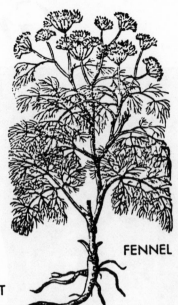

FENNEL

(MAKES 3 LOAVES)

1/2 CUP BUTTER OR MARGARINE

4 CUPS MILK, SCALDED

1/2 CUP BROWN SUGAR

1/2 CUP MOLASSES

1 TEASPOON ANISE SEED

1 TEASPOON FENNEL SEED

2 TABLESPOONS GRATED ORANGE PEEL

1 TABLESPOON SALT

2 CUPS RYE FLOUR

1 PACKAGE ACTIVE DRY YEAST

1/3 CUP WARM WATER

8 CUPS UNBLEACHED WHITE FLOUR

MELT BUTTER IN HEAVY SAUCEPAN. ADD 2 CUPS OF THE MILK, THE SUGAR, MOLAS-SES, ANISE AND FENNEL SEED, THE ORANGE PEEL AND SALT. ADD THE RYE FLOUR AND STIR OVER MEDIUM HEAT TO HEAT THOROUGHLY.

POUR INTO MIXING BOWL AND ADD REMAINING 2 CUPS MILK. COOL TO LUKEWARM. COMBINE YEAST AND WARM WATER. STIR TO DISSOLVE YEAST AND LET STAND 5 MIN-UTES. STIR INTO COOLED RYE FLOUR MIXTURE. STIR IN AS MUCH WHITE FLOUR AS YOU CAN, THEN KNEAD IN THE REST. CONTINUE KNEADING UNTIL DOUGH IS SMOOTH AND ELASTIC.

PLACE DOUGH IN GREASED BOWL AND TURN TO GREASE TOP. COVER AND LET RISE UNTIL DOUBLED IN BULK. PUNCH DOWN AND SHAPE INTO 3 LOAVES. PLACE IN GREASED 8 x 4-INCH LOAF PANS. COVER AND LET RISE TO TOPS OF PANS. BAKE IN PRE-HEATED 375° OVEN 45 MINUTES OR UNTIL BROWNED AND LOAVES SOUND HOLLOW WHEN TAPPED. REMOVE FROM PANS AND COOL ON RACKS.

Mary Murphy's Swedish Rye Bread

Honey Wheat Bread

(MAKES 2 LOAVES)

1 CUP BULGAR

3 TABLESPOONS BUTTER OR MARGARINE

1-1/2 CUPS BOILING WATER

1-1/4 CUPS COLD WATER

2 TEASPOONS SALT

1/2 CUP HONEY

1 PACKAGE ACTIVE DRY YEAST

3/4 CUP WARM WATER

3 CUPS STONE-GROUND WHOLE WHEAT FLOUR

3 CUPS UNBLEACHED WHITE FLOUR

COMBINE BULGAR, BUTTER AND BOILING WATER IN BOWL. LET STAND 30 MINUTES. STIR IN COLD WATER, SALT AND HONEY.

COMBINE YEAST AND WARM WATER. STIR TO BLEND AND LET STAND 5 MINUTES. ADD TO BULGAR MIXTURE. STIR IN WHOLE WHEAT FLOUR AND ENOUGH WHITE FLOUR TO MAKE A DOUGH THAT CAN BE HANDLED. TURN OUT ON FLOURED SURFACE AND KNEAD UNTIL SMOOTH AND ELASTIC.

PLACE DOUGH IN GREASED BOWL AND TURN TO COAT DOUGH. COVER AND LET RISE UNTIL DOUBLED IN BULK. PUNCH DOWN AND SHAPE INTO LOAVES. PLACE IN 2 GREASED 8 x 4-INCH LOAF PANS. COVER AND LET RISE UNTIL DOUGH RISES TO TOPS OF PANS. BAKE IN PRE-HEATED 375° OVEN ABOUT 45 MINUTES, OR UNTIL BREAD IS BROWNED AND LOAVES SOUND HOLLOW WHEN TAPPED ON THE BOTTOM. REMOVE FROM PANS AND COOL ON RACKS.

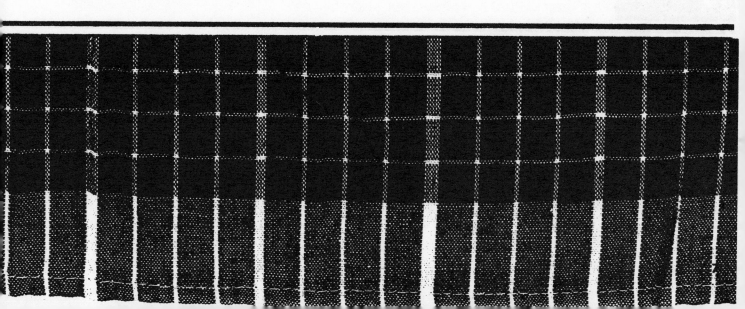

Oatmeal Bread

(MAKES 3 LOAVES)

1 CUP REGULAR OATS
1 CUP BOILING WATER
3 TABLESPOONS BUTTER OR MARGARINE
1 CUP COLD WATER
3/4 CUP MOLASSES

2 TEASPOONS SALT
1 PACKAGE ACTIVE DRY YEAST
3/4 CUP WARM WATER
8 TO 10 CUPS UNBLEACHED FLOUR

COMBINE OATS, BOILING WATER AND BUTTER IN MIXING BOWL; STIR TO MELT BUTTER. ADD COLD WATER, MOLASSES AND SALT. COOL TO LUKEWARM, IF NECESSARY.

COMBINE THE YEAST AND WARM WATER. STIR TO DISSOLVE, THEN LET STAND FOR 5 MINUTES. ADD TO COOLED OAT MIXTURE. STIR IN AS MUCH FLOUR AS YOU CAN, THEN KNEAD IN THE REST. CONTINUE KNEADING UNTIL DOUGH IS SMOOTH AND ELASTIC.

PLACE DOUGH IN GREASED BOWL; TURN TO GREASE TOP. COVER AND LET RISE UNTIL DOUBLED IN BULK. PUNCH DOWN AND SHAPE INTO 3 LOAVES. PLACE IN GREASED 8 x 4-INCH LOAF PANS. COVER AND LET RISE UNTIL DOUGH REACHES TOPS OF PANS. BAKE IN PRE-HEATED 375° OVEN 45 MINUTES, OR UNTIL BREAD IS BROWNED AND LOAVES SOUND HOLLOW WHEN TAPPED. REMOVE FROM PANS AND COOL ON RACKS.

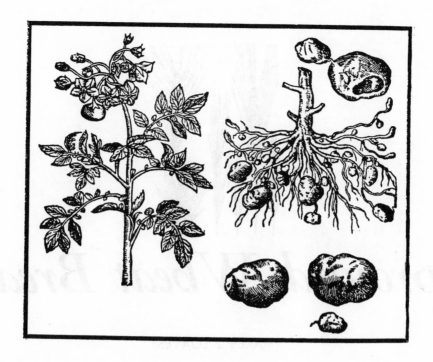

(MAKES 3 LOAVES)

9 CUPS UNBLEACHED FLOUR
1/4 CUP SHORTENING
2-1/4 CUPS POTATO WATER (LUKEWARM)*
5 TABLESPOONS SUGAR

2 PACKAGES ACTIVE DRY YEAST
1 CUP MILK, SCALDED
1 TABLESPOON SALT

BLEND 3 CUPS OF THE FLOUR WITH THE SHORTENING UNTIL EVENLY DIVIDED. SET ASIDE.

COMBINE POTATO WATER, HALF OF THE SUGAR, AND THE YEAST IN MIXING BOWL. STIR AND LET STAND 5 MINUTES TO DISSOLVE YEAST.

BLEND IN 3 CUPS OF THE FLOUR. LET RISE UNTIL DOUBLED IN BULK. STIR DOWN. ADD THE MILK (COOLED TO LUKEWARM), THE REMAINING SUGAR, AND THE SALT. ADD THE FLOUR-SHORTENING MIXTURE AND STIR IN AS MUCH OF THE REMAINING 3 CUPS OF FLOUR AS YOU CAN. KNEAD IN THE REST OF THE FLOUR UNTIL DOUGH IS SMOOTH.

PLACE IN GREASED BOWL; TURN TO COAT TOP AND LET RISE UNTIL DOUBLED. PUNCH DOWN AND SHAPE INTO 3 LOAVES. PLACE IN GREASED 8 x 4-INCH LOAF PANS. COVER AND LET RISE UNTIL DOUBLED. BAKE IN PRE-HEATED 375° OVEN FOR 40 TO 50 MINUTES, OR UNTIL BROWNED AND LOAVES SOUND HOLLOW WHEN TAPPED ON THE BOTTOM. REMOVE FROM PANS AND COOL ON RACKS.

* USE WATER IN WHICH POTATOES HAVE BEEN COOKED. OR MIX 1/4 CUP PUREED POTATOES WITH 2 CUPS WATER.

Potato Bread

Sprouted Wheat Bread

(MAKES 2 LOAVES)

1/2 CUP GROUND SPROUTED WHEAT*

3 CUPS WARM WATER

1 TABLESPOON SALT

3 TABLESPOONS VEGETABLE OIL

1/4 CUP HONEY

1 TEASPOON GRATED LEMON PEEL

1 PACKAGE ACTIVE DRY YEAST

4 CUPS STONE-GROUND WHOLE WHEAT FLOUR

4 CUPS UNBLEACHED WHITE FLOUR

COMBINE WHEAT SPROUTS, 2-1/4 CUPS WATER, THE SALT, OIL, HONEY, AND LEMON PEEL IN MIXING BOWL. ADD YEAST TO REMAINING 3/4 CUP WATER AND STIR TO DISSOLVE. LET STAND 5 MINUTES. ADD TO WHEAT SPROUT MIXTURE. STIR IN WHOLE WHEAT FLOUR AND AS MUCH WHITE FLOUR AS YOU CAN. KNEAD IN REST OF FLOUR. CONTINUE KNEADING UNTIL DOUGH IS SMOOTH AND ELASTIC.

PLACE DOUGH IN GREASED BOWL AND TURN TO GREASE TOP. COVER AND LET RISE UNTIL DOUBLED. PUNCH DOWN AND SHAPE INTO 2 LOAVES. PLACE IN GREASED 8 x 4-INCH LOAF PANS. COVER AND LET RISE UNTIL DOUGH RISES TO TOPS OF PANS. BAKE IN PRE-HEATED 375° OVEN ABOUT 1 HOUR, OR UNTIL BREAD IS BROWNED AND LOAVES SOUND HOLLOW WHEN TAPPED. REMOVE FROM PANS AND COOL ON RACKS.

* ONE FOURTH CUP OF WHEAT BERRIES WILL YIELD 2 CUPS OF WHEAT SPROUTS WHICH, IN TURN, WILL YIELD 1/2 CUP OF GROUND WHEAT SPROUTS. THE BEST DIRECTIONS I HAVE FOUND FOR SPROUTING WHEAT BERRIES AND OTHER SEEDS IS IN THE NEW YORK TIMES NATURAL FOODS COOKBOOK BY JEAN HEWITT.

Washington Wheat Bread

(MAKES 3 LOAVES)

3 CUPS WARM MILK

1/3 CUP BUTTER OR MARGARINE

1/3 CUP BROWN SUGAR

1/4 CUP MOLASSES

1/4 CUP SESAME SEED

3 TABLESPOONS CORNMEAL

2 EGGS, BEATEN

1 PACKAGE ACTIVE DRY YEAST

3/4 CUP WARM WATER

4-1/2 CUPS STONE-GROUND WHOLE
WHEAT FLOUR

1 TABLESPOON SALT

4 CUPS UNBLEACHED FLOUR

COMBINE MILK AND BUTTER; STIR TO MELT BUTTER. ADD SUGAR, MOLASSES, SESAME SEED, CORNMEAL AND EGGS. MIX WELL. COMBINE YEAST AND WATER; STIR TO DISSOLVE. LET STAND 5 MINUTES. STIR INTO MILK MIXTURE. ADD WHOLE WHEAT FLOUR AND STIR UNTIL BLENDED. LET RISE UNTIL DOUBLED.

STIR DOWN RISEN BATTER AND ADD SALT AND AS MUCH WHITE FLOUR AS YOU CAN STIR IN. KNEAD IN THE REST OF THE FLOUR. CONTINUE KNEADING UNTIL DOUGH IS SMOOTH AND ELASTIC. PLACE IN GREASED BOWL AND TURN TO GREASE TOP. COVER AND LET RISE UNTIL DOUBLED. PUNCH DOWN AND SHAPE INTO 3 LOAVES. PLACE IN GREASED 8 x 4-INCH LOAF PANS. COVER AND LET RISE UNTIL DOUGH RISES TO TOPS OF PANS. BAKE IN PRE-HEATED 375° OVEN 45 MINUTES, OR UNTIL BROWNED AND LOAVES SOUND HOLLOW WHEN TAPPED ON THE BOTTOM. REMOVE FROM PANS AND COOL ON RACKS.

Washington Wheat Bread

(MAKES 3 LOAVES)

1 PACKAGE ACTIVE DRY YEAST
3/4 CUP WARM WATER
4 1/2 CUPS STONE-GROUND WHOLE WHEAT FLOUR

Desserts

Dessert

ANYTIME YOU SEE DESSERTS TOPPED WITH PLASTIC-LOOKING WHIP
THEY DON'T CARE ENOUGH TO USE REAL WHIPPED CREAM, CHANCES
DESSERTS ARE WORTH THE CALORIES.

...oduction

...M COMING FROM A RESTAURANT'S KITCHEN, DON'T ORDER DESSERT. IF
... DESSERTS ARE AN AFTERTHOUGHT AND NOT WORTH THE CALORIES. OUR

Apple Crumb Pie

(MAKES 10-INCH PIE)

2/3 CUP GRANULATED SUGAR

2 TABLESPOONS FLOUR

1 TEASPOON CINNAMON

1/4 TEASPOON <u>EACH:</u> CLOVES, SALT
AND NUTMEG

6 CUPS COARSELY DICED, PEELED TART
APPLES

1 UNBAKED 10-INCH PIE SHELL

3/4 CUP FLOUR

1/2 CUP FIRMLY-PACKED BROWN SUGAR

6 TABLESPOONS BUTTER

1/3 CUP CHOPPED NUTS

COMBINE 2/3 CUP SUGAR, 2 TABLESPOONS FLOUR, THE SPICES AND SALT. TOSS TO-GETHER WITH DICED APPLES UNTIL WELL MIXED. SPOON INTO PIE SHELL. BAKE IN PRE-HEATED 400° OVEN FOR 25 MINUTES.

MEANWHILE, BLEND 3/4 CUP FLOUR WITH THE BROWN SUGAR UNTIL WELL BLENDED. CUT IN BUTTER UNTIL MIXTURE LOOKS LIKE COARSE MEAL. STIR IN NUTS. TAKE PIE FROM OVEN AND SPRINKLE WITH BUTTER-SUGAR MIXTURE. RETURN TO OVEN AND CONTINUE BAKING 30 TO 35 MINUTES, OR UNTIL BROWNED AND APPLES ARE TENDER.

Chocolate Cheesecake

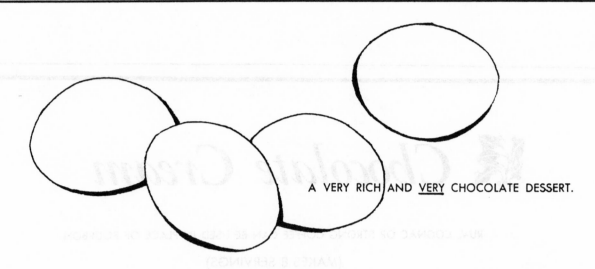

A VERY RICH AND <u>VERY</u> CHOCOLATE DESSERT.

(MAKES 10-INCH CAKE)

1-1/4 CUPS ZWIEBACK CRUMBS

1 TABLESPOON SUGAR

1/4 CUP MELTED BUTTER

12 OUNCES (12 SQUARES) SEMI-SWEET CHOCOLATE

1/2 CUP HOT COFFEE

2 PACKAGES (8 OUNCES EACH) CREAM CHEESE

1 CUP SUGAR

4 EGGS

2 TEASPOONS VANILLA

1/4 TEASPOON SALT

WHIPPED CREAM

SHAVED CHOCOLATE

COMBINE ZWIEBACK CRUMBS AND 1 TABLESPOON SUGAR. BUTTER SIDES OF 10-INCH SPRINGFORM PAN. SHAKE SOME OF CRUMBS AROUND PAN TO COAT SIDES. ADD MELTED BUTTER TO REST OF CRUMBS; BLEND WELL. PRESS OVER BOTTOM OF PAN.

MEANWHILE, MELT CHOCOLATE WITH COFFEE OVER HOT, NOT BOILING, WATER. BEAT CREAM CHEESE UNTIL LIGHT AND FLUFFY. GRADUALLY ADD SUGAR, BEATING CONSTANTLY. SCRAPE DOWN SIDES OF BOWL AND BEAT AGAIN. ADD EGGS, ONE AT A TIME, BEATING WELL AFTER EACH. STIR IN VANILLA AND SALT. BEAT IN MELTED CHOCOLATE UNTIL BLENDED. POUR INTO PREPARED PAN. BAKE IN PRE-HEATED 325° OVEN FOR 55 MINUTES. TURN OFF HEAT, SET OVEN DOOR AJAR AND LET COOL 2 TO 3 HOURS. BEFORE SERVING, SPREAD WITH WHIPPED CREAM AND SPRINKLE WITH SHAVED CHOCOLATE. CAKE IS BEST SERVED AT ROOM TEMPERATURE. REFRIGERATE FOR PROLONGED STORAGE.

 # *Chocolate Cream*

RUM, COGNAC OR STRONG COFFEE CAN BE USED IN PLACE OF BOURBON.

(MAKES 8 SERVINGS)

2 BARS (4 OUNCES EACH) GERMAN'S SWEET CHOCOLATE

6 TABLESPOONS BOURBON

2 TABLESPOONS WATER

6 TABLESPOONS SUGAR

2 CUPS HEAVY CREAM

1 TEASPOON VANILLA

COMBINE CHOCOLATE, BOURBON AND WATER IN SAUCEPAN. COVER AND PLACE OVER HOT, NOT BOILING, WATER UNTIL MELTED. STIR UNTIL SMOOTH. ADD SUGAR AND BLEND. STIR INTO HEAVY CREAM AND STIR UNTIL BLENDED. ADD VANILLA. CHILL SEVERAL HOURS OR OVERNIGHT. BEAT WITH ELECTRIC MIXER OR WIRE WHIP UNTIL STIFF. SPOON INTO POT DE CREME POTS OR CUSTARD CUPS. SERVE AT ONCE OR COVER AND FREEZE.

Creme Caramel

(MAKES 12 SERVINGS)

2 CUPS SUGAR

7 EGG YOLKS

5 WHOLE EGGS

4 CUPS MILK

1-1/3 CUPS HEAVY CREAM

2 TEASPOONS VANILLA

PUT 1 CUP OF THE SUGAR IN LARGE HEAVY SKILLET. STIR OVER MEDIUM HEAT UNTIL MELTED AND A MEDIUM BROWN. POUR INTO 2-1/2 QUART OVEN-PROOF DISH OR PAN. TILT PAN TO COVER BOTTOM WITH SYRUP.

MEANWHILE, COMBINE YOLKS AND WHOLE EGGS IN MIXING BOWL. BEAT UNTIL BLENDED. BEAT IN REMAINING 1 CUP OF SUGAR. SCALD MILK AND CREAM. SLOWLY BEAT INTO EGG MIXTURE. ADD VANILLA. POUR INTO PAN OVER CARAMELIZED SUGAR. SET IN PAN OF HOT WATER AND PLACE IN PRE-HEATED 350° OVEN. REDUCE HEAT TO 325° AND BAKE 1 HOUR, OR UNTIL KNIFE INSERTED IN CENTER COMES OUT CLEAN. COOL, THEN CHILL. IF DESIRED, RUN A SHARP KNIFE AROUND EDGE AND UNMOLD.

THIS IS NOT THE EASIEST DESSERT TO MAKE BUT IT'S ONE OF THE BEST. THE RECIPE COMES FROM THE COACH HOUSE RESTAURANT IN NEW YORK CITY. THE MERINGUE LAYERS TEND TO TURN SOGGY IN HOT, HUMID WEATHER SO WE RARELY SERVE IT DURING THE SUMMER. AND, IF YOU DON'T HAVE AN ELECTRIC MIXER, YOU'D BETTER HAVE A STRONG ARM AND LOTS OF ENDURANCE.

Dacquoise

(MAKES 12 SERVINGS)

5 EGGS, SEPARATED

DASH SALT

1/8 TEASPOON CREAM OF TARTAR

2-1/4 CUPS SUGAR

1 CUP GROUND ALMONDS

1/2 CUP ZWIEBACK CRUMBS

2 TABLESPOONS FLOUR

2 TABLESPOONS CORNSTARCH

1/2 TEASPOON VANILLA

1/3 CUP WATER

1-1/4 CUPS UNSALTED BUTTER, AT ROOM TEMPERATURE

2 TABLESPOONS INSTANT COFFEE

2 TABLESPOONS COINTREAU OR GRAND MARNIER

CONFECTIONERS SUGAR

SHAVED SEMI-SWEET CHOCOLATE

MARK TWO 9-INCH CIRCLES ON A SHEET OF BAKING PARCHMENT PAPER. OR MARK THE CIRCLES ON WAXED PAPER, THEN GREASE AND FLOUR THE CIRCLES. SET ASIDE.

PUT 5 EGG WHITES IN LARGE BOWL OF ELECTRIC MIXER WITH A DASH OF SALT. BEAT UNTIL FOAMY. ADD CREAM OF TARTAR AND CONTINUE BEATING UNTIL SOFT PEAKS BEGIN TO FORM. GRADUALLY ADD 3/4 CUP OF THE SUGAR, BEATING CONSTANTLY. CONTINUE BEATING UNTIL MIXTURE WILL STAND IN STIFF PEAKS.

MEANWHILE, COMBINE ALMONDS, CRUMBS, 1/2 CUP OF THE SUGAR, THE FLOUR, CORNSTARCH AND VANILLA; MIX UNTIL WELL BLENDED. GENTLY FOLD INTO BEATEN EGG WHITES. SPREAD MIXTURE EVENLY IN CIRCLES DRAWN ON PAPER. BAKE IN PRE-HEATED 250° OVEN FOR 45 MINUTES. COOL, THEN LOOSEN FROM PAPER WITH A SPATULA.

TO MAKE FILLING, COMBINE REMAINING 1 CUP OF THE SUGAR AND THE WATER IN SAUCEPAN. STIR OVER MEDIUM HEAT UNTIL SUGAR DISSOLVES. BRING TO A BOIL AND COVER FOR 2 TO 3 MINUTES. UNCOVER AND BOIL UNTIL SYRUP REACHES A TEMPERATURE OF 236° OR UNTIL SYRUP SPINS A DEFINITE THREAD.

MEANWHILE, BEAT 5 EGG YOLKS WITH ELECTRIC MIXER UNTIL THICK AND LEMON COLORED. WHILE BEATING YOLKS CONSTANTLY, START ADDING BOILING SYRUP GRADUALLY. WHEN ALL OF THE SYRUP HAS BEEN ADDED, BEGIN ADDING BUTTER. ADD IT 2 TABLESPOONS AT A TIME, STILL BEATING CONSTANTLY. THEN, BEAT IN A MIXTURE OF INSTANT COFFEE AND COINTREAU. CHILL MIXTURE 4 TO 6 HOURS, THEN BEAT UNTIL STIFF ENOUGH TO HOLD ITS SHAPE.

SPREAD BETWEEN COOLED MERINGUE LAYERS. LIGHTLY SPRINKLE CONFECTIONERS SUGAR AND SHAVED CHOCOLATE ON TOP. CHILL.

Elli Fenn's Cheesecake

CINNAMON

THIS IS A DENSE CHEESECAKE. WE LIKE IT SLIGHTLY UNDERBAKED SO THAT IT SLUMPS JUST A LITTLE IN THE CENTER WHEN IT'S CUT.

(MAKES 9- OR 10-INCH CAKE)

1-1/4 CUPS ZWIEBACK CRUMBS

3 TABLESPOONS SUGAR

1/4 TEASPOON CINNAMON

1/4 CUP MELTED BUTTER

5 PACKAGES (8 OUNCES EACH) CREAM CHEESE, SOFTENED

1-3/4 CUPS SUGAR

3 TABLESPOONS FLOUR

1/4 TEASPOON SALT

2 TEASPOONS VANILLA

2 TEASPOONS GRATED LEMON PEEL

6 EGGS

1/4 CUP HEAVY CREAM

COMBINE CRUMBS, 3 TABLESPOONS OF THE SUGAR, AND THE CINNAMON. MIX WELL. BUTTER SIDES OF A 9- OR 10-INCH SPRINGFORM PAN. SHAKE A LITTLE OF THE CRUMB MIXTURE IN PAN TO COAT SIDES. BLEND BUTTER INTO REMAINING CRUMBS. RESERVE 1/4 CUP CRUMBS FOR TOPPING. PRESS REMAINING CRUMBS OVER BOTTOM OF SPRINGFORM PAN.

MEANWHILE, BEAT CREAM CHEESE IN LARGE BOWL WITH ELECTRIC MIXER UNTIL FLUFFY. GRADUALLY BEAT IN A MIXTURE OF SUGAR, FLOUR AND SALT. ADD VANILLA AND LEMON PEEL. ADD EGGS ONE AT A TIME, BEATING WELL AFTER EACH. BEAT IN CREAM. POUR BATTER INTO CRUMB-LINED PAN AND SPRINKLE RESERVED CRUMBS OVER TOP. BAKE IN PRE-HEATED 300° OVEN FOR 1 HOUR. TURN OFF OVEN AND COOL IN OVEN WITH DOOR AJAR 2 TO 3 HOURS. CAKE SHOULD STILL BE SOFT IN THE CENTER. CHILL.

Engadine Torte

THIS IS A GREAT DO-AHEAD DESSERT. IT KEEPS WELL, BAKED OR UNBAKED, AND FREEZES BEAUTIFULLY.

(MAKES 12 SERVINGS)

2-1/2 CUPS SUGAR

1 CUP HEAVY CREAM

2-1/2 CUPS BROKEN WALNUTS

1 CUP BUTTER

1 EGG

2-3/4 CUPS FLOUR

1 EGG WHITE, LIGHTLY BEATEN

PLACE 2 CUPS OF THE SUGAR IN LARGE HEAVY SKILLET. STIR OVER MEDIUM HEAT WITH A WOODEN SPOON UNTIL SUGAR MELTS COMPLETELY AND TURNS A DEEP GOLDEN BROWN. ADD CREAM ALL AT ONCE. STIR CAREFULLY AS MIXTURE WILL STEAM AND BUBBLE FURIOUSLY. STIR UNTIL COMBINED, THEN MIX IN WALNUTS. SET ASIDE TO COOL TO ROOM TEMPERATURE.

BEAT BUTTER WITH ELECTRIC MIXER UNTIL LIGHT AND FLUFFY. GRADUALLY ADD REMAINING 1/2 CUP OF THE SUGAR. BEAT IN EGG. GRADUALLY BLEND IN FLOUR.

MEASURE 2 CUPS OF DOUGH INTO 9-, 10-, OR 11-INCH TORTE PAN (WITH REMOVABLE SIDES). PRESS DOUGH EVENLY OVER BOTTOM AND SIDES OF PAN. SPOON COOLED NUT MIXTURE INTO PAN. CHILL.

SHAPE REMAINING DOUGH (ABOUT 1 CUP) INTO A FLAT ROUND. PLACE BETWEEN 2 SHEETS OF WAXED PAPER AND ROLL OUT LARGE ENOUGH TO FIT OVER NUT FILLING IN TORTE PAN. CHILL ABOUT 1 HOUR. PEEL OFF 1 SHEET OF PAPER AND CENTER OVER NUT FILLING. PEEL OFF OTHER SHEET OF PAPER. PRESS EDGES TOGETHER TO SEAL, AND PINCH OFF ANY EXCESS. MAKE A DESIGN ALONG EDGE WITH TINES OF A FORK. PRICK TOP WITH THE FORK AND BRUSH WITH BEATEN EGG WHITE. BAKE IN PRE-HEATED 350° OVEN FOR 45 TO 60 MINUTES, OR UNTIL WELL BROWNED. COOL. CUT IN WEDGES TO SERVE.

WALNUT

Freeman Allen's Carrot Cake

THIS IS AN EASY AND ALMOST FOOL-PROOF CAKE.

(MAKES 9 x 13-INCH CAKE)

2 CUPS FLOUR	1-1/4 CUPS VEGETABLE OIL
2 CUPS SUGAR	3 CUPS GRATED CARROTS
2 TEASPOONS BAKING POWDER	4 EGGS
2 TEASPOONS BAKING SODA	1/2 CUP CHOPPED NUTS
1 TEASPOON SALT	2 TEASPOONS VANILLA
2 TEASPOONS CINNAMON	CREAM CHEESE FROSTING

COMBINE FLOUR, SUGAR, BAKING POWDER, SODA, SALT AND CINNAMON IN LARGE BOWL OF MIXER. MIX UNTIL WELL BLENDED, ABOUT 3 TO 4 MINUTES.

ADD OIL TO FLOUR MIXTURE WHILE MIXING. THEN ADD THE CARROTS AND THE EGGS ONE AT A TIME, MIXING WELL AFTER EACH. STIR IN NUTS AND VANILLA. MIX WELL. POUR INTO GREASED AND FLOURED 9 x 13-INCH PAN. BAKE IN PRE-HEATED 350° OVEN 50 TO 60 MINUTES, OR UNTIL CAKE SPRINGS BACK WHEN LIGHTLY TOUCHED. COOL IN PAN. FROST WITH CREAM CHEESE FROSTING.

CREAM CHEESE FROSTING

(MAKES ABOUT 1-1/2 CUPS)

4 OUNCES CREAM CHEESE	2 CUPS CONFECTIONERS SUGAR (ABOUT)
1/4 CUP BUTTER	

COMBINE CHEESE AND BUTTER IN SMALL MIXER BOWL. BEAT UNTIL LIGHT AND FLUFFY. ADD CONFECTIONERS SUGAR AND BEAT TO BLEND. USE ADDITIONAL SUGAR, IF NECESSARY. SPREAD ON TOP OF CARROT CAKE.

French Chocolate Cake

AS FAR AS WE KNOW, THIS CAKE WORKS ONLY WITH MAILLARD CHOCOLATE, WHICH MUST BE MELTED SLOWLY. THE CAKE IS LIGHTER AND MORE DELICATE IF THE BUTTER IS BEATEN UNTIL FLUFFY WITH AN ELECTRIC MIXER BUT YOU CAN USE SOFTENED (ROOM TEMPERATURE) BUTTER.

(MAKES 8-INCH CAKE)

1 POUND MAILLARD EAGLE SWEET CHOCOLATE

10 TABLESPOONS BUTTER

1 TABLESPOON SUGAR

1 TABLESPOON FLOUR

4 EGGS, SEPARATED

1 TABLESPOON WATER

DASH SALT

WHIPPED CREAM

LINE BOTTOM AND SIDES OF AN 8- OR 9-INCH SPRINGFORM PAN WITH WAXED PAPER; SET ASIDE.

SET CHOCOLATE IN A BOWL OVER HOT, <u>NOT BOILING</u>, WATER SO THAT CHOCOLATE MELTS VERY SLOWLY. MEANWHILE, BEAT BUTTER UNTIL LIGHT AND FLUFFY.

WHEN CHOCOLATE IS MELTED, REMOVE FROM HEAT AND COOL SLIGHTLY. STIR IN SUGAR AND FLOUR. THEN STIR IN BUTTER. BEAT EGG YOLKS LIGHTLY WITH THE WATER. BLEND INTO CHOCOLATE MIXTURE. ADD A DASH OF SALT TO EGG WHITES. BEAT UNTIL STIFF PEAKS FORM BUT MIXTURE IS STILL MOIST AND SHINY LOOKING. FOLD QUICKLY AND EVENLY INTO CHOCOLATE MIXTURE. POUR INTO PREPARED PAN. BAKE IN PRE-HEATED 425° OVEN 15 MINUTES. TURN OFF HEAT AND ALLOW CAKE TO COOL IN OVEN WITH DOOR AJAR. CAKE IS BEST SERVED AT ROOM TEMPERATURE. JUST BEFORE SERVING, TOP WITH WHIPPED CREAM.

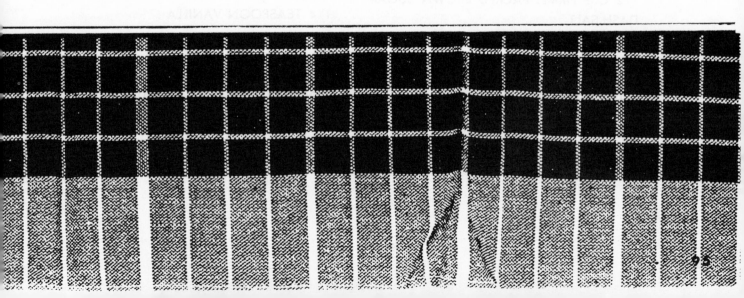

Fresh Apple Cake

(MAKES 9 x 13-INCH CAKE)

2-1/3 CUPS FLOUR

2 CUPS SUGAR

2 TEASPOONS BAKING SODA

3/4 TEASPOON SALT

1 TEASPOON CINNAMON

1/4 TEASPOON <u>EACH</u>: CLOVES AND
    NUTMEG

4 CUPS CHOPPED, PEELED APPLES

1/2 CUP SOFT SHORTENING

1/2 CUP CHOPPED WALNUTS

2 EGGS

CARAMEL FROSTING

    COMBINE FLOUR, SUGAR, SODA, SALT AND SPICES IN LARGE MIXING BOWL. MIX UNTIL WELL BLENDED, 3 TO 4 MINUTES.

    ADD APPLES, SHORTENING, NUTS AND EGGS. BEAT AT MEDIUM SPEED UNTIL WELL BLENDED. POUR INTO A GREASED AND FLOURED 9 x 13-INCH PAN. BAKE IN PRE-HEATED 325° OVEN 45 MINUTES, OR UNTIL CAKE SPRINGS BACK WHEN TOUCHED. COOL COMPLETELY ON WIRE RACK. FROST IN PAN WITH CARAMEL FROSTING.

CARAMEL FROSTING

(MAKES ABOUT 1 CUP)

1/3 CUP BUTTER

1/2 CUP FIRMLY-PACKED BROWN SUGAR

DASH SALT

3 TABLESPOONS MILK

1-1/2 CUPS SIFTED CONFECTIONERS
    SUGAR (ABOUT)

1/4 TEASPOON VANILLA

    MELT BUTTER IN SMALL SAUCEPAN. ADD BROWN SUGAR AND SALT. STIR OVER MEDIUM HEAT UNTIL SUGAR MELTS. ADD MILK AND BRING TO A BOIL. POUR INTO MIXING BOWL AND COOL 10 MINUTES. ADD CONFECTIONERS SUGAR AND VANILLA. BEAT TO SPREADING CONSISTENCY, ADDING ADDITIONAL CONFECTIONERS SUGAR, IF NECESSARY. SPREAD ON FRESH APPLE CAKE.

Fresh Rhubarb Pie

(MAKES 10-INCH PIE)

6 CUPS DICED FRESH RHUBARB

2 CUPS SUGAR

1/4 CUP MINUTE TAPIOCA

1/4 TEASPOON SALT

2 TABLESPOONS MELTED BUTTER

PASTRY FOR DOUBLE-CRUST PIE

COMBINE RHUBARB, SUGAR, TAPIOCA, SALT AND BUTTER; LET STAND 20 MINUTES.

POUR RHUBARB FILLING INTO PASTRY-LINED PIE PAN. CENTER TOP CRUST OVER FILL-ING. SEAL AND FLUTE EDGE. CUT VENTS IN TOP CRUST AND BRUSH LIGHTLY WITH CREAM AND SPRINKLE WITH GRANULATED SUGAR. BAKE IN PRE-HEATED 400° OVEN FOR 45 MIN-UTES, OR UNTIL FILLING BUBBLES VIGOROUSLY IN THE CENTER OF THE PIE AND THE CRUST IS WELL BROWNED. COOL 2 TO 3 HOURS BEFORE CUTTING.

Fruit Fool

1/2 POUND CURRANTS,
   BLACKBERRIES, OR
   RHUBARB

2/3 CUP SUGAR

1-1/2 CUPS HEAVY CREAM

CONFECTIONERS SUGAR

(MAKES ABOUT 6 SERVINGS)

COMBINE WASHED FRUIT AND SUGAR. LET STAND A FEW MINUTES FOR JUICE TO FORM. STIR OVER LOW HEAT UNTIL MIXTURE BOILS. SIMMER OVER LOW HEAT, STIRRING FREQUENTLY, FOR 10 MINUTES.

REMOVE FROM HEAT AND PUT FRUIT THROUGH A FOOD MILL OR FORCE THROUGH A STRAINER TO MAKE A SMOOTH PUREE. (SKIP THIS STEP FOR RHUBARB.) CHILL THOR-OUGHLY.

WHIP CREAM UNTIL SOFT PEAKS FORM. DEPENDING UPON TARTNESS OF FRUIT, SWEETEN CREAM WITH 1/4 TO 1/2 CUP OF CONFECTIONERS SUGAR. FOLD IN CHILLED FRUIT PUREE SO THAT FRUIT STREAKS THROUGH CREAM. SERVE IN CHILLED BOWLS.

Half-Baked Chocolate Mousse

(MAKES 8 SERVINGS)

8 OUNCES SEMI-SWEET CHOCOLATE *

1/4 CUP HOT COFFEE

FINE DRY BREAD CRUMBS

8 EGGS, SEPARATED

2/3 CUP GRANULATED SUGAR

2 TEASPOONS VANILLA

DASH SALT

1 CUP HEAVY CREAM

3 TABLESPOONS CONFECTIONERS SUG

1/4 TEASPOON VANILLA

PLACE CHOCOLATE IN A BOWL AND SET OVER HOT, NOT BOILING, WATER. PC HOT COFFEE OVER CHOCOLATE AND LET MELT. WHEN ALMOST MELTED, STIR U BLENDED AND SMOOTH.

BUTTER A 9- OR 10-INCH PIE PLATE AND COAT WITH FINE DRY BREAD CRUMBS GRAHAM CRACKER CRUMBS. SET ASIDE.

PLACE EGG YOLKS IN MIXING BOWL AND BEAT UNTIL THICK AND LEMON COLOR ADD GRANULATED SUGAR GRADUALLY, BEATING CONSTANTLY. BEAT IN 2 TEASPOO VANILLA, THEN THE MELTED CHOCOLATE.

ADD A DASH OF SALT TO EGG WHITES. BEAT WHITES WITH ROTARY BEATER OR EL TRIC MIXER UNTIL WHITES ARE STIFF BUT STILL MOIST AND GLOSSY. ADD ABOUT 1/4 BEATEN WHITES INTO CHOCOLATE MIXTURE. STIR UNTIL WELL BLENDED. CAREFULLY FC IN REMAINING EGG WHITES. POUR ABOUT HALF OF CHOCOLATE MIXTURE INTO PREPAF PAN. BAKE IN 350° OVEN FOR 25 MINUTES. TURN OFF OVEN HEAT AND LEAVE IN OVEI MINUTES. REMOVE FROM OVEN AND COOL COMPLETELY. (CENTER WILL SINK.)

MEANWHILE CHILL REMAINING CHOCOLATE MIXTURE 2 TO 3 HOURS, OR OVERNIG SPOON INTO THE MIDDLE OF BAKED CHOCOLATE MOUSSE.

WHIP CREAM UNTIL ALMOST STIFF. ADD CONFECTIONERS SUGAR AND 1/4 T SPOON VANILLA. BEAT UNTIL STIFF. SPREAD OVER TOP AND CHILL UNTIL SERVED.

* USE 8 ONE-OUNCE SQUARES OF SEMI-SWEET CHOCOLATE. THIS RECIPE DOES N WORK WITH CHOCOLATE CHIPS.

Joe's Sister's Cheesecake

(MAKES 10-INCH CAKE)

/2 CUPS ZWIEBACK CRUMBS (ABOUT 3/4 BOX)

TABLESPOONS SUGAR

4 CUP MELTED BUTTER

PACKAGES (8 OUNCES EACH) CREAM CHEESE, SOFTENED

/4 CUPS SUGAR

TABLESPOONS FLOUR

3/4 TEASPOON GRATED LEMON RIND

6 EGGS, SEPARATED

1 PINT SOUR CREAM

1 TEASPOON VANILLA

DASH SALT

2 TABLESPOONS SUGAR

BUTTER SIDES OF A 10-INCH SPRINGFORM PAN; COAT WITH A MIXTURE OF ZWIE-CK CRUMBS AND 3 TABLESPOONS SUGAR. COMBINE REMAINING CRUMBS AND MELTED TTER; BLEND WELL. RESERVE 1/4 CUP BUTTERED CRUMBS. PAT REMAINING CRUMBS ER BOTTOM OF PAN. SET ASIDE.

BEAT CHEESE UNTIL LIGHT AND FLUFFY. BLEND 1-1/4 CUPS SUGAR AND THE FLOUR ID GRADUALLY BEAT INTO CHEESE. ADD LEMON RIND AND EGG YOLKS, ONE AT A AE, BEATING WELL AFTER EACH. BLEND IN SOUR CREAM AND VANILLA.

ADD SALT TO EGG WHITES AND BEAT UNTIL SOFT PEAKS FORM. ADD 2 TABLESPOONS GAR, BEATING CONSTANTLY. BEAT UNTIL STIFF. CAREFULLY FOLD INTO CHEESE MIXTURE. UR INTO PREPARED PAN. SPRINKLE RESERVED CRUMBS ON TOP. BAKE IN A PRE-HEATED 5° OVEN FOR 1 HOUR. TURN OFF HEAT IN OVEN AND SET OVEN DOOR AJAR. LET COOL OVEN COMPLETELY, 3 TO 4 HOURS. CHILL THOROUGHLY BEFORE SERVING.

Kentucky Pecan Pie

(MAKES 9- OR 10-INCH PIE)

4 EGGS, BEATEN

2/3 CUP FIRMLY-PACKED DARK BROWN SUGAR

1/4 TEASPOON SALT

1-1/3 CUPS LIGHT CORN SYRUP

1/4 CUP MELTED BUTTER

1/2 TEASPOON VANILLA

1-1/3 CUPS BROKEN PECANS

9- OR 10-INCH UNBAKED PIE SHELL

COMBINE EGGS AND SUGAR IN MIXING BOWL. BEAT UNTIL BLENDED. ADD SALT, SYRUP, BUTTER, VANILLA AND PECANS. MIX WELL. POUR INTO PIE SHELL. BAKE IN PRE-HEATED 400° OVEN FOR 15 MINUTES. REDUCE HEAT TO 350° AND CONTINUE BAKING 25 TO 35 MINUTES, OR UNTIL SET IN CENTER. COOL BEFORE SERVING.

Key Lime Pie

(MAKES 9-INCH PIE)

1-1/2 CUPS GRAHAM CRACKER CRUMBS

2 TABLESPOONS SUGAR

1/2 CUP MELTED BUTTER

4 EGGS, SEPARATED

1 CAN (14 OUNCES) SWEETENED CONDENSED MILK

1/2 CUP LIME JUICE

1 TEASPOON GRATED LIME PEEL

GREEN FOOD COLORING (OPTIONAL)

DASH SALT

1/4 TEASPOON CREAM OF TARTAR

1/2 CUP SUGAR

TO MAKE CRUST, COMBINE CRUMBS AND 2 TABLESPOONS SUGAR; MIX WELL. BLEND IN BUTTER. PRESS OVER BOTTOM AND SIDES OF 9-INCH PIE PLATE. BAKE IN PRE-HEATED 350° OVEN FOR 10 MINUTES. COOL THOROUGHLY.

BEAT EGG YOLKS LIGHTLY IN MIXING BOWL. BLEND IN SWEETENED CONDENSED MILK. STIR IN LIME JUICE AND LIME PEEL. TINT A PALE GREEN WITH FOOD COLORING, IF DESIRED. POUR INTO COOLED CRUST.

ADD A DASH OF SALT TO THE EGG WHITES AND BEAT WITH A ROTARY BEATER UNTIL FOAMY. ADD CREAM OF TARTAR AND CONTINUE BEATING UNTIL VERY SOFT PEAKS START TO FORM. ADD 1/2 CUP SUGAR GRADUALLY, 2 TABLESPOONS AT A TIME, BEATING CON-STANTLY. CONTINUE BEATING UNTIL STIFF PEAKS FORM. SPREAD MERINGUE OVER TOP OF PIE TO THE EDGE OF CRUST. BAKE IN PRE-HEATED 450° OVEN 5 TO 8 MINUTES, OR UNTIL MERINGUE IS BROWNED. COOL COMPLETELY BEFORE CUTTING.

Mintry's Miracle

(MAKES 8 TO 10 SERVINGS)

1 CUP UNSALTED BUTTER

1 CUP SUPERFINE SUGAR

6 EGGS, SEPARATED

2 OUNCES (2 SQUARES) UNSWEETENED
CHOCOLATE

1/4 CUP BOURBON

24 AMARETTI MACAROONS

1 TEASPOON VANILLA

1/2 CUP CHOPPED TOASTED PECANS

12 DOUBLE LADY FINGERS

DASH SALT

1 CUP HEAVY CREAM

BEAT BUTTER WITH ELECTRIC MIXER UNTIL VERY LIGHT AND FLUFFY. ADD SUGAR GRAD-UALLY, BEATING CONSTANTLY.

MEANWHILE, SEPARATE EGGS AND BEAT EGG YOLKS UNTIL LIGHT AND PALE YELLOW IN COLOR. MELT CHOCOLATE OVER HOT, NOT BOILING, WATER. SPRINKLE BOURBON OVER AMARETTI MACAROONS.

BEAT EGG YOLKS INTO BUTTER MIXTURE. THEN STIR IN MELTED CHOCOLATE, THE VANILLA, AND PECANS.

LINE A 9-INCH SQUARE PAN WITH SPLIT LADY FINGERS. ADD A DASH OF SALT TO EGG WHITES. BEAT UNTIL STIFF BUT NOT DRY. FOLD INTO CHOCOLATE-BUTTER MIXTURE. SPOON HALF OF THIS OVER LADY FINGERS AND SPREAD EVENLY. ARRANGE MACAROONS EVENLY OVER CHOCOLATE MIXTURE. SPREAD REMAINING CHOCOLATE MIXTURE OVER MACAROONS. CHILL SEVERAL HOURS OR OVERNIGHT.

WHIP CREAM UNTIL STIFF. SWEETEN TO TASTE, IF DESIRED. SPREAD OVER TOP AND CHILL UNTIL SERVING TIME.

Mocha Macaroon Pie

1-1/4 CUPS GRAHAM CRACKER CRUMBS

6 OUNCES (1-1/3 BARS) GERMAN'S SWEET CHOCOLATE

2/3 CUP CHOPPED TOASTED PECANS

1 CUP SUGAR

1 TEASPOON BAKING POWDER

DASH SALT

5 EGG WHITES

2 TEASPOONS VANILLA

1/2 TEASPOON WATER

2 TEASPOONS INSTANT COFFEE

1 CUP HEAVY CREAM

1/4 CUP CONFECTIONERS SUGAR

CRUSH CRACKERS TO MAKE CRUMBS. GRATE CHOCOLATE, AND RESERVE 2 TABLESPOONS FOR TOPPING. CHOP TOASTED NUTS. BUTTER A 10-INCH PIE PAN THOROUGHLY. HEAT OVEN TO 350°.

MIX 1 CUP SUGAR THOROUGHLY WITH BAKING POWDER. ADD SALT TO EGG WHITES IN LARGE MIXER BOWL. BEAT WITH ELECTRIC MIXER UNTIL VERY SOFT PEAKS START TO FORM. START ADDING SUGAR GRADUALLY WHILE BEATING CONSTANTLY. CONTINUE BEATING A MINUTE OR TWO AFTER ALL SUGAR IS ADDED. ADD CRACKER CRUMBS, GRATED CHOCOLATE, NUTS AND 1 TEASPOON OF THE VANILLA TO EGG WHITES AND CAREFULLY FOLD IN. SPOON INTO BUTTERED PIE PAN. BAKE IN 350° OVEN 30 TO 35 MINUTES, OR UNTIL BROWNED. COOL THOROUGHLY.

ADD WATER AND REMAINING 1 TEASPOON OF VANILLA TO INSTANT COFFEE AND STIR TO DISSOLVE. BLEND INTO HEAVY CREAM WITH CONFECTIONERS SUGAR. CHILL SEVERAL HOURS.

ABOUT 1 HOUR BEFORE SERVING, WHIP CREAM UNTIL STIFF. SPREAD OVER CENTER OF PIE. SPRINKLE RESERVED CHOCOLATE OVER CREAM. CHILL UNTIL READY TO SERVE.

Pumpkin Pie

(MAKES 10-INCH PIE)

10-INCH UNBAKED PIE SHELL
2 TEASPOONS MELTED BUTTER
2 CUPS COOKED OR CANNED PUMPKIN
3/4 CUP FIRMLY-PACKED DARK BROWN
  SUGAR
1 TEASPOON SALT
1 TEASPOON CINNAMON

1 TEASPOON GINGER
1/4 TEASPOON NUTMEG
1 CUP MILK, SCALDED
1 SMALL CAN (2/3 CUP) EVAPORATED
  MILK
3 EGGS, BEATEN

BRUSH PIE SHELL WITH MELTED BUTTER AND CHILL 30 MINUTES OR LONGER.

COMBINE PUMPKIN, SUGAR, SALT AND SPICES IN SAUCEPAN. COOK, STIRRING FRE-
QUENTLY, UNTIL THICK. STIR IN MILKS AND EGGS. BEAT UNTIL BLENDED.

PRE-HEAT OVEN TO 425°. BAKE PIE FOR 15 MINUTES. REDUCE HEAT TO 350° AND CON-
TINUE BAKING 45 MINUTES, OR UNTIL KNIFE INSERTED IN CENTER COMES OUT CLEAN.
COOL. SERVE WITH SWEETENED WHIPPED CREAM.

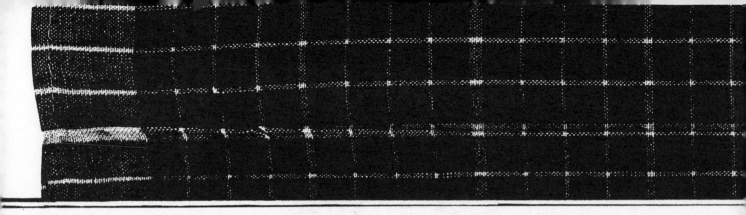

Sugar Pie

(MAKES 9-INCH PIE)

1 CUP FIRMLY-PACKED DARK BROWN
  SUGAR (8 OUNCES)

6 TABLESPOONS FLOUR

9-INCH UNBAKED PIE SHELL

1 CUP HEAVY CREAM

1-1/2 CUPS LIGHT CREAM

1 TEASPOON VANILLA

2 TABLESPOONS BUTTER

COMBINE SUGAR AND FLOUR; MIX TOGETHER VERY WELL. SPREAD EVENLY IN PIE SHELL.

COMBINE HEAVY AND LIGHT CREAMS AND VANILLA. POUR EVENLY OVER SUGAR IN PIE SHELL. DOT TOP WITH BUTTER. BAKE IN 400° OVEN FOR 10 MINUTES. REDUCE HEAT TO 350° AND CONTINUE BAKING FOR 40 MINUTES, OR UNTIL FILLING BUBBLES ALL OVER AND BEGINS TO SET IN CENTER. COOL BEFORE SERVING.

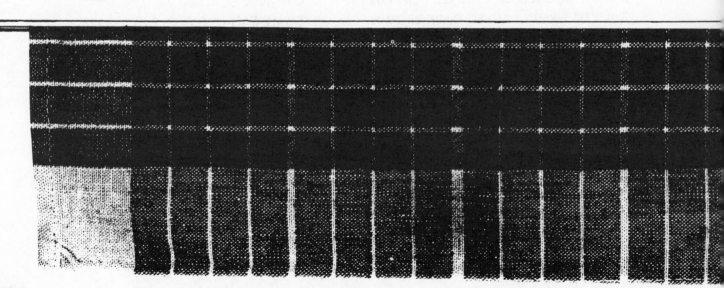

Raisin-Nut Pie

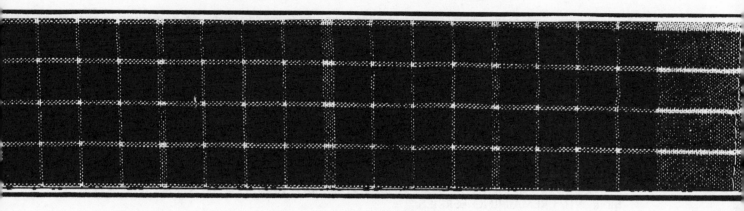

(MAKES 9-INCH PIE)

1-1/4 CUPS SEEDLESS RAISINS

2/3 CUP BROKEN WALNUTS

1/2 TEASPOON GRATED LEMON PEEL

1-1/2 TABLESPOONS LEMON JUICE

1/2 CUP BUTTER

2/3 CUP GRANULATED SUGAR

1/3 CUP FIRMLY-PACKED BROWN SUGAR

1 TEASPOON CINNAMON

1/4 TEASPOON SALT

3 EGGS

UNBAKED 9-INCH PIE SHELL

COMBINE RAISINS, NUTS AND LEMON PEEL AND JUICE. SET ASIDE.

BEAT BUTTER UNTIL LIGHT AND FLUFFY. BEAT IN SUGARS, CINNAMON AND SALT. ADD EGGS, ONE AT A TIME, BEATING WELL AFTER EACH. STIR IN RAISIN MIXTURE. SPOON INTO PIE SHELL. BAKE IN PRE-HEATED 400° OVEN 15 MINUTES. REDUCE HEAT TO 350° AND CONTINUE BAKING 20 MINUTES, OR UNTIL SET IN CENTER. COOL.

Raspberry Flummery

THIS RECIPE WILL WORK WITH ANY TART BERRY AND PROBABLY WITH OTHER FRUITS TOO.

(MAKES 6 SERVINGS)

1 QUART FRESH RASPBERRIES
1 CUP SUGAR
2 TABLESPOONS WATER

10-12 SLICES DAY-OLD HOMEMADE TYPE BREAD
6 TABLESPOONS MELTED BUTTER
1 CUP HEAVY CREAM

COMBINE 1/2 CUP RASPBERRIES, THE SUGAR AND THE WATER IN SAUCEPAN. BRING TO A BOIL OVER MEDIUM HEAT, STIRRING FREQUENTLY. SIMMER 3 TO 4 MINUTES. COMBINE WITH REMAINING BERRIES.

MEANWHILE, TRIM CRUSTS FROM BREAD AND BRUSH BUTTER ON BOTH SIDES OF SLICES. LINE BOTTOM OF 8- OR 9-INCH SQUARE PAN WITH THE BREAD. SPOON SOME OF THE BERRIES OVER BREAD AND TOP WITH MORE BREAD. CONTINUE LAYERING, ENDING WITH BREAD. COVER WITH PLASTIC WRAP. WEIGHT TOP WITH HEAVY POT AND CHILL OVERNIGHT. WHIP CREAM, SWEETEN TO TASTE, AND SPREAD ON TOP OF DESSERT. CUT INTO SQUARES TO SERVE.

BLUEBERRY FLUMMERY

FOLLOW DIRECTIONS FOR STRAWBERRY FLUMMERY, SUBSTITUTING WILD BLUEBERRIES FOR STRAWBERRIES AND OMITTING CINNAMON.

 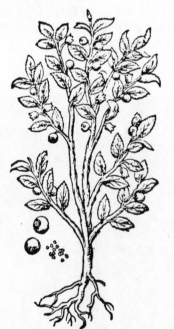 

STRAWBERRY FLUMMERY

USE FRESH STRAWBERRIES IN PLACE OF RASPBERRIES. COMBINE ALL OF THE BERRIES WITH THE SUGAR AND WATER AND A DASH OF BOTH CINNAMON AND CLOVES. PROCEED AS DIRECTED IN RASPBERRY FLUMMERY RECIPE.

Pie Pastry Mix

6-3/4 CUPS UNBLEACHED FLOUR
1 TABLESPOON SALT

3/4 CUP VEGETABLE SHORTENING
1-1/2 CUPS LARD

MEASURE FLOUR AND SALT INTO MIXING BOWL. STIR UNTIL WELL BLENDED. CUT IN SHORTENING UNTIL MIXTURE RESEMBLES CORNMEAL. THEN CUT IN LARD UNTIL MIXTURE RESEMBLES SMALL PEAS. STORE IN COVERED CONTAINER IN REFRIGERATOR.

TO MAKE 9- OR 10-INCH PIE SHELL: MEASURE 1-1/2 CUPS MIX INTO MIXING BOWL. SPRINKLE WITH 2-1/2 TABLESPOONS ICE WATER WHILE TOSSING MIX WITH A FORK. GATHER INTO A BALL AND FLATTEN INTO A SMOOTH ROUND. ROLL OUT ON FLOURED SURFACE INTO A ROUND 1-1/2 INCHES LARGER THAN INVERTED PIE PAN. ROLL PASTRY ONTO ROLLING PIN TO TRANSFER TO PAN. FIT INTO PIE PAN AND TRIM EDGES 1/2 INCH BEYOND EDGE. FORM A STANDING RIM AND FLUTE. IF SHELL IS TO BE BAKED, PRICK WITH A FORK AND PLACE IN 425° OVEN ABOUT 15 MINUTES.

TO MAKE DOUBLE CRUST PIE: MEASURE 2-1/4 CUPS PASTRY INTO MIXING BOWL. SPRINKLE WITH 3-1/2 TABLESPOONS ICE WATER WHILE TOSSING MIX WITH A FORK. GATHER INTO A BALL AND DIVIDE IN HALF. FOLLOW ABOVE DIRECTIONS FOR ROLLING OUT. AFTER PASTRY IS FITTED INTO PAN, TRIM EVEN WITH EDGE. ROLL OUT REMAINING HALF OF PASTRY TO 1 INCH BEYOND EDGE OF INVERTED PIE PAN. ADD FILLING TO PASTRY-LINED PAN. CENTER ROLLED-OUT PASTRY OVER FILLING AND TRIM 1/2 INCH BEYOND EDGE. FOLD TOP CRUST UNDER BOTTOM AND PINCH TOGETHER. FLUTE AND BAKE AS DIRECTED.

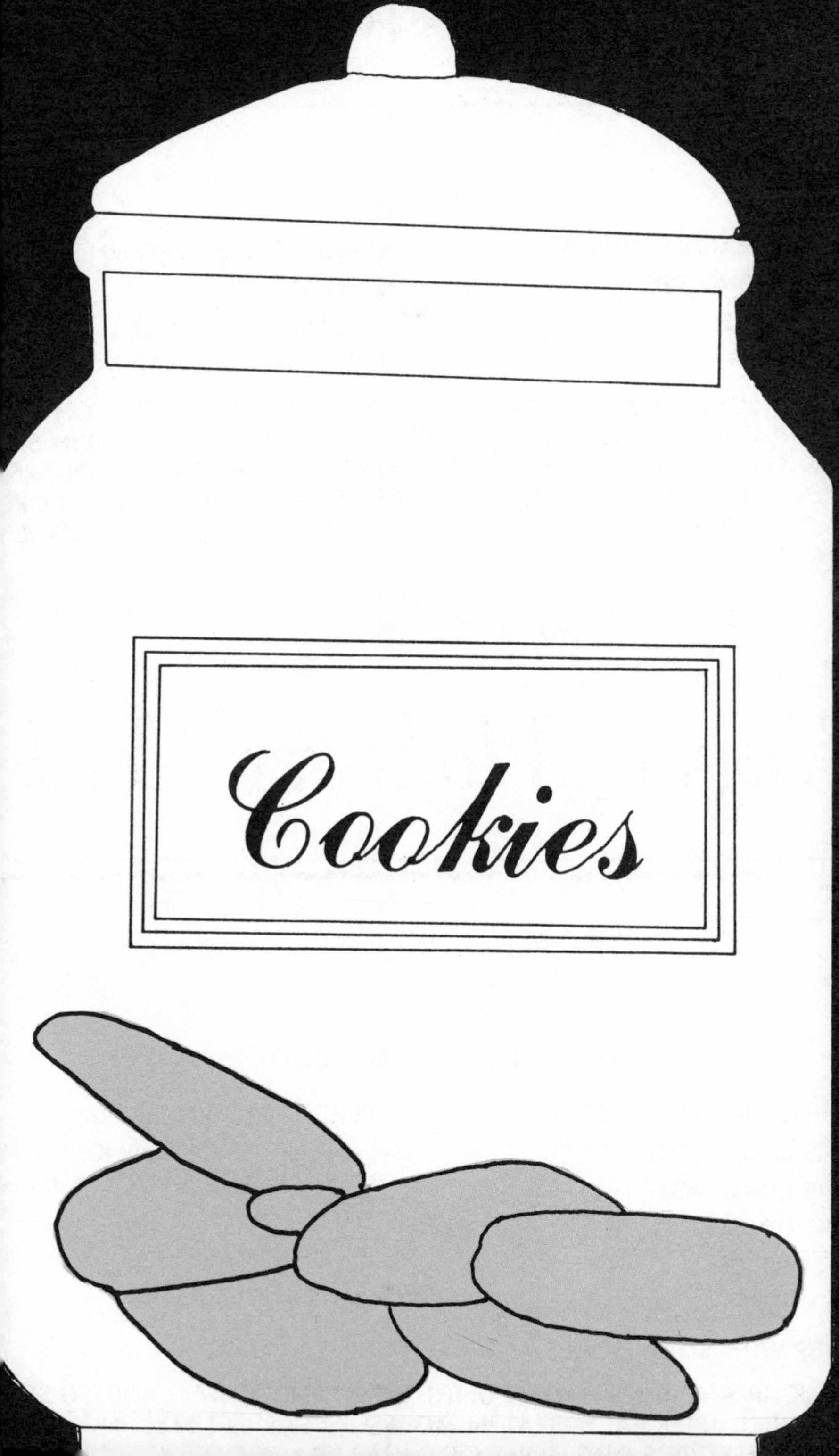
Cookies

Butter-Nut Chip Cookies

(MAKES 50 COOKIES)

3-1/2 CUPS UNBLEACHED FLOUR

1 TEASPOON BAKING SODA

1/2 TEASPOON SALT

1/2 POUND BUTTER

1 POUND DARK BROWN SUGAR

2 EGGS

1 TEASPOON VANILLA

1 CUP BROKEN WALNUTS

SIFT FLOUR, SODA AND SALT TOGETHER. CREAM BUTTER UNTIL LIGHT. ADD SUGAR AND BEAT UNTIL LIGHT AND FLUFFY. BEAT IN EGGS ONE AT A TIME. STIR IN SIFTED INGREDIENTS, THEN THE VANILLA AND NUTS. SHAPE INTO A LONG 1-INCH ROLL AND WRAP IN WAXED PAPER. CHILL UNTIL FIRM. CUT INTO VERY THIN SLICES. PLACE ON GREASED BAKING SHEET. BAKE IN PRE-HEATED 375° OVEN 10 TO 12 MINUTES, OR UNTIL BROWNED. COOL ON RACKS.

Ginger Molasses Cookies

(MAKES ABOUT 50 LARGE COOKIES)

4-1/2 CUPS UNBLEACHED FLOUR

4 TEASPOONS BAKING SODA

2 TEASPOONS CINNAMON

4 TEASPOONS GINGER

1 TEASPOON CLOVES

1/2 TEASPOON SALT

1 POUND BROWN SUGAR

1-1/2 CUPS SHORTENING, OR MIXTURE OF LARD AND SHORTENING

2 EGGS

1/2 CUP MOLASSES

GRANULATED SUGAR

SIFT FLOUR WITH SODA, SPICES AND SALT.

CREAM SUGAR AND SHORTENING UNTIL LIGHT AND FLUFFY. ADD EGGS ONE AT A TIME, BEATING WELL AFTER EACH. BEAT IN MOLASSES. STIR IN SIFTED INGREDIENTS. DROP BY ROUNDED TABLESPOONS INTO BOWL OF SUGAR. PLACE ON GREASED BAKING SHEET, SUGAR-SIDE UP, ABOUT 2 INCHES APART. BAKE IN PRE-HEATED 375° OVEN ABOUT 15 MINUTES. COOL ON RACKS.

Oatmeal Cookies

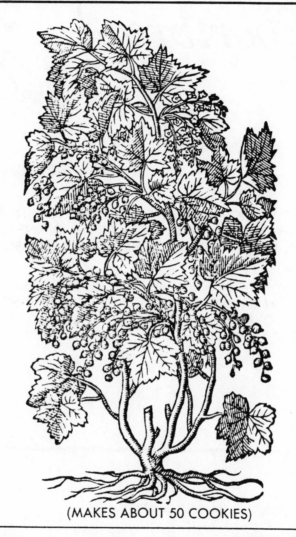

(MAKES ABOUT 50 COOKIES)

3 CUPS REGULAR OATS

1 CUP GRANULATED SUGAR

1 CUP FIRMLY-PACKED BROWN SUGAR

3 CUPS UNBLEACHED FLOUR

1 TEASPOON CINNAMON

1 TEASPOON SALT

1 CUP RAISINS

1 CUP VEGETABLE OIL

2 EGGS

1 3 CUP MILK

1 TEASPOON BAKING SODA

COMBINE OATS, SUGARS, FLOUR, CINNAMON AND SALT; MIX VERY WELL. STIR IN RAISINS. MIX IN OIL, THEN EGGS, ONE AT A TIME. COMBINE MILK AND SODA AND BLEND INTO DOUGH. MIX WELL. DROP BY ROUNDED TABLESPOONS ONTO GREASED COOKIE SHEET. BAKE IN PRE-HEATED 375° OVEN 15 TO 20 MINUTES, OR UNTIL BROWNED. COOL ON RACKS.

Scotch Shortbread

SUGAR CANE

(MAKES ABOUT 50 COOKIES)

2-1/2 CUPS BUTTER

1-1/2 CUPS SUGAR

6 CUPS UNBLEACHED FLOUR

BEAT BUTTER WITH ELECTRIC MIXER UNTIL VERY LIGHT AND FLUFFY. GRADUALLY BEAT IN SUGAR, BEATING CONSTANTLY. STIR IN FLOUR TO BLEND. KNEAD DOUGH ON LIGHTLY FLOURED SURFACE UNTIL DOUGH "BREAKS" WHEN THUMB IS RUBBED LIGHTLY OVER THE SURFACE.

MEASURE OUT ABOUT 1/2 CUP PORTIONS OF DOUGH. SHAPE INTO FLAT ROUNDS ABOUT 1/2 INCH THICK ON BAKING SHEETS. FLUTE EDGES AND SCORE INTO QUARTERS. BAKE IN PRE-HEATED 300° OVEN FOR 30 MINUTES, OR UNTIL VERY LIGHTLY BROWNED AROUND EDGES. REMOVE FROM OVEN AND IMMEDIATELY CUT ALONG SCORE LINES. COOL ON RACKS.

Brownies

(MAKES 24 BROWNIES)

1 CUP BUTTER OR MARGARINE

4 SQUARES (4 OUNCES) UNSWEETENED
CHOCOLATE

2 CUPS SUGAR

4 EGGS

1 CUP UNBLEACHED FLOUR

1 CUP BROKEN WALNUTS

COMBINE BUTTER AND CHOCOLATE IN SAUCEPAN. MELT OVER LOW HEAT, STIRRING OCCASIONALLY. STIR IN SUGAR, THEN BEAT IN EGGS, ONE AT A TIME. STIR IN FLOUR, THEN THE NUTS. POUR INTO A WELL-GREASED 9 x 12-INCH PAN. BAKE IN PRE-HEATED 375° OVEN 20 TO 25 MINUTES. COOL AND CUT INTO SQUARES.

Date and Oatmeal Bars

(MAKES 25 BARS)

3/4 POUND PITTED DATES, CUT UP

6 TABLESPOONS SUGAR

2/3 CUP WATER

3 TABLESPOONS LEMON JUICE

1/2 CUP BROKEN WALNUTS

1-1/2 CUPS UNBLEACHED FLOUR

1/2 TEASPOON BAKING SODA

1/2 TEASPOON SALT

3/4 CUP BUTTER OR MARGARINE

1 CUP FIRMLY-PACKED DARK BROWN SUGAR

2 CUPS REGULAR OATS

COMBINE DATES, SUGAR AND WATER IN SAUCEPAN. BRING TO A BOIL AND SIMMER OVER LOW HEAT 10 MINUTES, STIRRING FREQUENTLY. COOL. STIR IN LEMON JUICE AND WALNUTS.

SIFT FLOUR, BAKING SODA AND SALT TOGETHER. CREAM BUTTER UNTIL LIGHT. ADD SUGAR AND CONTINUE BEATING UNTIL LIGHT AND FLUFFY. STIR IN SIFTED INGREDIENTS, THEN THE OATS.

PRESS ABOUT 2/3 OF THE OAT MIXTURE INTO BOTTOM OF GREASED 9 x 12-INCH PAN. TOP WITH DATE MIXTURE AND SPREAD EVENLY. SPRINKLE WITH REMAINING OAT MIXTURE AND PAT LIGHTLY. BAKE IN PRE-HEATED 375° OVEN FOR 30 TO 35 MINUTES. COOL IN PAN. CUT INTO BARS.

Sangría

(MAKES 4 SERVINGS)

1/2 ORANGE, SLICED	2 TABLESPOONS COINTREAU
1/2 LEMON, SLICED	3 CUPS DRY RED WINE
1/2 APPLE, SLICED	ICE
2 TABLESPOONS SUGAR	

COMBINE FRUIT, SUGAR AND COINTREAU IN LARGE PITCHER. LET STAND FOR 30 MINUTES TO 1 HOUR. ADD WINE AND STIR TO DISSOLVE SUGAR. ADD ICE AND SERVE AT ONCE.

Hot Mulled Wine

(MAKES 5 CUPS)

3/4 CUP SUGAR	2 TWO-INCH PIECES LEMON PEEL
1/2 CUP WATER	2 TWO-INCH PIECES ORANGE PEEL
1/2 TEASPOON WHOLE CLOVES	1 QUART DRY RED WINE
2 STICKS CINNAMON	

COMBINE SUGAR, WATER, SPICES AND FRUIT PEELS IN SAUCEPAN. BRING TO A BOIL AND SIMMER 5 MINUTES. ADD WINE AND HEAT TO JUST BELOW BOILING POINT. STRAIN AND SERVE AT ONCE.

Soup Bowl Paté Maison

(MAKES ABOUT 1-1/4 POUNDS)

1/2 POUND BUTTER, SOFTENED	2 PINCHES THYME
3/4 CUP SLICED SCALLIONS	1 PINCH NUTMEG
1 MEDIUM CLOVE GARLIC, MINCED	1-1/2 TEASPOONS DRY MUSTARD
1 POUND CHICKEN LIVERS	10 GRINDS PEPPER
3 TABLESPOONS COGNAC	SALT TO TASTE (DEPENDS ON SALTINESS
1 PINCH MACE	OF BUTTER)
1 PINCH CLOVES	

HEAT 3 TABLESPOONS BUTTER IN SKILLET. ADD SCALLIONS AND GARLIC AND SAUTE UNTIL JUST TENDER. REMOVE FROM SKILLET. ADD ANOTHER 2 TABLESPOONS BUTTER TO SKILLET AND HEAT. SAUTE LIVERS A FEW AT A TIME JUST UNTIL THEY BEGIN TO FEEL FIRM TO THE TOUCH. THEY SHOULD BE TAKEN FROM THE SKILLET WHILE STILL QUITE PINK IN THE CENTER.

AFTER ALL LIVERS ARE COOKED, ADD COGNAC TO SKILLET AND SCRAPE OFF BROWNED BITS. HEAT COGNAC, THEN LIGHT IT. WHEN FLAME DIES DOWN, POUR OVER LIVERS.

CHOP ABOUT 1/3 OF THE LIVERS COARSELY; SET ASIDE. PUT REMAINING LIVERS IN BLENDER JAR WITH REMAINING BUTTER AND THE SPICES. BLEND UNTIL VERY SMOOTH. COMBINE BLENDED MIXTURE, THE CHOPPED LIVERS AND THE SCALLIONS. MIX WELL AND SEASON TO TASTE WITH SALT. POUR INTO MOLD AND CHILL UNTIL FIRM. UNMOLD AND SLICE TO SERVE.

Quiche

Quiche Introduction

CUSTOMERS TEND TO PRESSURE RESTAURANT OWNERS TO EXPAND THEIR MENUS. PERHAPS THAT'S HOW THOSE ENORMOUSLY LARGE AND WEIGHTY MENUS CAME INTO EXISTENCE. SOME POOR SOUL WAS TOO WEAK TO RESIST THE WELL-INTENTIONED PRESSURE.

UNTIL NOW WE HAVE RESISTED SUCH PRESSURE (MOSTLY REQUESTS TO ADD SANDWICHES TO OUR BILL OF FARE). IN PART OUR STERN RESISTANCE RESULTED FROM THE CHEF'S AVERSION TO SANDWICH-MAKING. SHE FINDS IT A BORE. BUT WE DID SUCCUMB WHERE QUICHE IS CONCERNED BECAUSE WE BELIEVE WE HAVE DEVELOPED SOME EXCELLENT RECIPES.

Betty White's Mexican Quiche

(MAKES 8 SERVINGS)

10-INCH UNBAKED PIE SHELL

2 TABLESPOONS MELTED BUTTER

8 OUNCES CREAM CHEESE, DICED

2 CANS (4 OUNCES EACH) GREEN CHILIES, DRAINED

5 EGGS

1-1/2 CUPS HEAVY CREAM

1/2 TEASPOON SALT

DASH PEPPER

1 CUP SHREDDED SWISS, CHEDDAR OR JACK CHEESE

BRUSH PIE SHELL WITH BUTTER AND ARRANGE CREAM CHEESE OVER THE BOTTOM. CHILL UNTIL BUTTER IS SET.

MEANWHILE, SPREAD CHILIES ON PAPER TOWELS TO DRAIN THOROUGHLY. IF WHOLE CHILIES ARE USED, CHOP COARSELY.

COMBINE EGGS, CREAM AND SEASONINGS; BEAT UNTIL BLENDED. SPRINKLE CHILIES OVER CREAM CHEESE IN PIE SHELL AND TOP WITH SHREDDED CHEESE. POUR EGG MIXTURE EVENLY OVER ALL. BAKE IN PRE-HEATED 425° OVEN FOR 15 MINUTES. REDUCE HEAT TO 350° AND CONTINUE BAKING 30 MINUTES, OR UNTIL KNIFE INSERTED IN CENTER COMES OUT CLEAN. COOL 5 TO 10 MINUTES BEFORE CUTTING.

Fritata

(MAKES 8 SERVINGS)

3/4 CUP CHOPPED GREEN PEPPER

1-1/2 CUPS SLICED MUSHROOMS

1-1/2 CUPS CHOPPED ZUCCHINI

3/4 CUP CHOPPED ONION

1 LARGE CLOVE GARLIC, MINCED

3 TABLESPOONS OIL

6 EGGS, BEATEN

1/4 CUP LIGHT CREAM

1 POUND CREAM CHEESE, DICED

1-1/2 CUPS SHREDDED CHEDDAR CHEESE

2 CUPS CUBED BREAD

1 TEASPOON SALT

1/4 TEASPOON PEPPER

SAUTE GREEN PEPPER, MUSHROOMS, ZUCCHINI, ONION AND GARLIC IN OIL UNTIL ZUCCHINI IS CRISP-TENDER. COOL SLIGHTLY.

BEAT EGGS WITH CREAM. ADD CREAM CHEESE, CHEDDAR CHEESE, BREAD, SALT, PEPPER AND SAUTEED VEGETABLES. MIX WELL. POUR INTO GREASED 10-INCH SPRING-FORM PAN. BAKE IN PRE-HEATED 350° OVEN FOR 1 HOUR OR UNTIL SET IN CENTER. COOL 10 MINUTES BEFORE CUTTING.

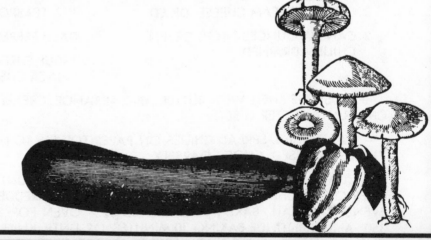

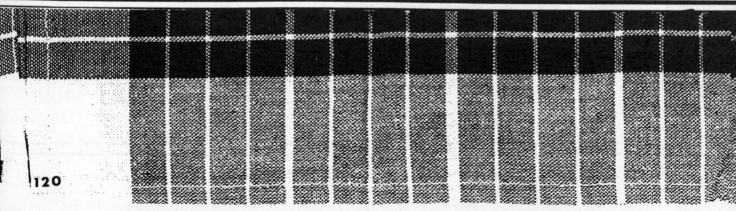

Spinach Quiche

(MAKES 8 SERVINGS)

3/4 CUP CHOPPED GREEN PEPPER

3/4 CUP CHOPPED ONION

1-1/2 CUPS SLICED MUSHROOMS

1-1/2 CUPS CHOPPED ZUCCHINI

1-1/2 TEASPOONS MINCED GARLIC

3 TABLESPOONS VEGETABLE OIL

5 EGGS

1 POUND RICOTTA CHEESE

1 TEASPOON SALT

1/8 TEASPOON PEPPER

10 OUNCES SPINACH, COOKED AND CHOPPED

1 CUP CRUMBLED FETA CHEESE OR GRATED CHEDDAR CHEESE

SAUTE GREEN PEPPER, ONION, MUSHROOMS, ZUCCHINI AND GARLIC IN OIL UNTIL CRISP-TENDER. COOL.

BEAT EGGS WITH RICOTTA CHEESE, SALT AND PEPPER. DRAIN SPINACH THOROUGHLY, SQUEEZING AS MUCH MOISTURE OUT AS POSSIBLE. ADD TO EGG MIXTURE ALONG WITH SAUTEED VEGETABLES AND FETA CHEESE. MIX UNTIL WELL BLENDED.

POUR SPINACH MIXTURE INTO A GREASED 10-INCH SPRING-FORM PAN AND SPREAD EVENLY. BAKE IN PRE-HEATED 350° OVEN 1 HOUR OR UNTIL SET IN CENTER. COOL 10 MINUTES BEFORE CUTTING.

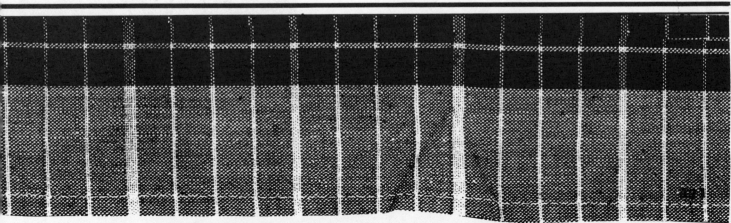

Deb Venman's Tomato Quiche

(MAKES 8 SERVINGS)

10-INCH UNBAKED PIE SHELL

2 TABLESPOONS MELTED BUTTER

1/2 CUP GRATED PARMESAN CHEESE

2 CUPS WELL-DRAINED CUBED PEELED TOMATOES (FRESH OR CANNED)

3 TABLESPOONS FLOUR

4 WHOLE EGGS

2 EGG YOLKS

1 CUP HEAVY CREAM

1/2 CUP TOMATO JUICE

3/4 TEASPOON WORCESTERSHIRE

1/2 CUP MINCED SCALLIONS

1/2 TEASPOON SALT

DASH PEPPER

1/4 TEASPOON NUTMEG

1 CUP SHREDDED SWISS OR CHEDDAR CHEESE

BRUSH PIE SHELL WITH BUTTER AND SPRINKLE WITH PARMESAN CHEESE. CHILL. COMBINE TOMATOES AND FLOUR; SET ASIDE.

COMBINE EGGS, EGG YOLKS, CREAM, TOMATO JUICE, WORCESTERSHIRE, SCALLIONS, SALT, PEPPER AND NUTMEG. BEAT UNTIL BLENDED.

SPREAD TOMATOES OVER PARMESAN CHEESE IN PIE SHELL AND TOP WITH SHREDDED CHEESE. POUR EGG MIXTURE EVENLY OVER INGREDIENTS IN PIE SHELL. BAKE IN PREHEATED 425° OVEN FOR 15 MINUTES. REDUCE HEAT TO 350° AND CONTINUE BAKING 30 TO 40 MINUTES, OR UNTIL KNIFE INSERTED IN CENTER COMES OUT CLEAN. COOL 5 TO 10 MINUTES BEFORE CUTTING.

index

index

index

index

index

index